James

A Commentary and an Exposition of the Book of James
for Teen and Adult Bible Study

Charley D. Ward

ONESTONE
BIBLICAL RESOURCES

Published by:
One Stone Press
979 Lovers Lane
Bowling Green, KY 42103

Printed in the United States of America

All biblical references are based upon the
King James Version unless otherwise noted.

ISBN: 978-1-941422-52-6

ONE STONE
BIBLICAL RESOURCES
www.onestone.com

Contents

Lesson   **Page**

Preface 5

I. 1:1-8 11

II. 1:9-17 21

III. 1:18-25 31

IV. 1:26-27; 2:1-7 39

V. 2:8-13 49

VI. 2:14-26 55

VII. 3:1-12 65

VIII. 3:13-18; 4:1-3 77

IX. 4: 4-10 85

X. 4:11-17 91

XI. 5:1-12 97

XII. 5:13-20 109

Bibliography 118

Preface

This study of the Epistle of James intends to aid the Bible student, both young and old. The twelve lessons contain commentary on the text and discussion questions for study and review. Each student should understand that this is a commentary written to be an aid or study guide with easy to follow comments on each verse of the five chapters of this epistle. By understanding each verse of this marvelous epistle, students can learn how to practice "pure and undefiled religion" before God.

In no way should one study or use this workbook as if it exhausts the subjects set forth by James, the inspired writer. My discussion stems from gathering notes from sermons and Bible studies over many years. I will attempt to offer my understanding of the Book of James to "rightly dividing the word of truth" and assist the Bible student who is seeking a better understanding of each verse of this Epistle (2 Timothy 2:15). Having a greater understanding of each passage will allow one to make the proper application in their daily walk of life.

Every Christian should desire a better understanding of the "perfect law of liberty" contained in the Book of James. This study attempts to aid the "newborn babe" in Christ as well as those who have a deeper understanding of the Scriptures. Cross-referencing other passages of Scripture will enlighten the young in the faith as well as the older Christian. Thus all age groups can read, study, meditate, understand, and apply the Biblical principles set forth in the Holy Scriptures.

The Book of James gives insight into God's instructions for practical, godly living to help the reader understand and make the proper application enabling faithful Christians to stay in the race set before them. An understanding of the benefits of afflictions, trials, and persecutions will help believers to endure faithfully until the end.

The instructions outlined in James' epistle to those of the early church still apply to the saints today. These God-inspired instructions found in the Epistle of James teach us how we are to entreat one another as brethren and will edify us until the end of time. Therefore, open your Bibles and pray to God for understanding as you study this epistle.

The Book of James is as relevant and needful today in godly living as it was needful to the early saints converted from Judaism to Christianity. The early church in Jerusalem was scattered abroad in the first century due to persecution and needed instruction concerning faith, works, and perseverance in all of life's struggles so they could continue to be obedient believers in Christ. Every time I have studied this epistle it strengthens my faith and helps me endure temptations in the form of trials as well as temptations in the form of allurements to sin. James gives thorough instructions on how to avoid the misuse of the tongue. If a Christian bridles his/her tongue, then he/she can bring the whole body into subjection.

By using other Scriptures written by various inspired writers, we can better our understanding of how God would have us live faithfully in our corrupt society. When one studies these passages of James and then compares them to similar passages in other epistles, it will also bring to mind our Lord's teaching as he instructed His disciples. It seems to me that when James writes to the brethren scattered because of persecution, he seems to exemplify the Lord's instructions in His ministry, especially in the Sermon on the Mount.

This study reflects my sincere desire to ascertain and present the precise thoughts the inspired writer James desired to communicate to individuals of the early church and thus give insight and understanding for our edification today. I will be using the King James Version (KJV) primarily because it is one of the most reliable translations that faithful men and women have used for centuries. I will refer to other versions of the Bible, such as the American Standard Version (ASV) and possibly different versions, as noted for clarity and understanding. Also, I will reference various Bible scholars and their comments as to their knowledge of the meaning of these Scriptures. I will often quote W.E. Vine's Dictionary of N.T. Words regarding the meaning of the original Greek words which will aid our understanding of what James is saying to his readers. Should I quote other Bible scholars' writings, I will attempt to give credit where credit is due by acknowledging their scholarly work with references concerning their understanding, comments, and writings.

I am humbly praying the Lord's blessing upon this feeble attempt to promote the cause of Christ by rightly dividing the word of truth, which James refers to as "the perfect law of liberty." I have surpassed the 74th milepost in my life's journey. I am not sure I will be able to complete such an undertaking of this magnitude, but should I fail to achieve this endeavor, I will still prosper even more by my deeper understanding of this marvelous epistle. My heart desires to continue teaching and preaching the good word of God until I draw my last breath. Should I fail to finish this workbook due to health reasons, I will, nonetheless, devote my time and effort to the ministry of Jesus Christ in the allotted time which God has given me. If this workbook helps one soul to cross the finish line faithfully, then it will not have been in vain.

A Brief Summary Of What Is And What Is Not Contained In The Epistle Of James

In all my years of study, I have never found an entire book in the New Testament, which addresses the day-to-day struggles of Christians like this epistle does. Every exhortation James offers to the scattered abroad saints remains just as applicable to us today. I am amazed at how practical this book is to everyday godly living in the Twenty-first Century. Everyone needs to study and make proper application to their life.

The message of this book will hurt one's feelings, step on one's toes, but at the same time, it will strengthen one's faith beyond measure. So be prepared to receive "with meekness the engrafted word which is able to save your souls" (James 1:21). When studying a passage from the inspired text, realize God is speaking through divine inspiration. When one's conscience condemns, then instantly go to God in prayer and confess to Him their faults and shortcomings. One must always be willing to make changes according to what was just learned. It is no wonder Bible students appropriately refer to this epistle as "the N.T. book of proverbs" and also the "gospel of common sense."

James gives admonishment to God's people, which will enable the sincere followers of Christ to withstand the temptations of life and to resist the devil in their daily lives. This letter advises one to persevere during the trials of faith, to not show partiality of the rich over the poor, to bridle the tongue, to not be quarrelsome or greedy, to prac

tice patience, and to know the power of prayer. Be prepared to say "AMEN" or "OUCH" as James speaks directly to you in his letter.

What The Book Of James Does Not Specifically Address

This general Epistle of James is not a book containing examples of conversions. James addresses those already converted to Christ. It is not a book containing the miracles of Christ to prove His deity, nor a discussion of the birth, life, ministry, death, burial, and resurrection of our Lord. It does not focus on subjects like partaking of the Lord's supper, giving, establishing Bible authority, and singing; neither does it provide doctrinal instruction on the scriptural worship and work of the N.T church. It does not focus on the events of the Day of Judgement but does allude to Christ's Second Coming. Neither does it focus on the resurrection of the just and the unjust in detail. This letter is not addressed to a specific church at one location but rather to individual believers in general. However, it focuses merely on the individual's faith and how an obedient believer is to live godly in this present world. As the theme suggests, it admonishes the first-fruits of his creatures (1:18) to practice pure and undefiled religion before God.

Who Is The Writer Of This Epistle?

The first word of this book identifies the writer by name. James identifies himself as a servant of God and the Lord Jesus Christ. Since "James" is found some 40 times in the New Testament, the controversy is which James is the penman of this epistle. Among those mentioned, several could be the writer. Here are a few possibilities:

(1) James, the son of Zebedee, one of the 12 Apostles (Matt. 4:21; 10:2-4; Mark 3:17; Luke 6:14, Acts 1:2-3). Matthew mentions him with his brother (Matt. 4:21 and 17:1). Mark 3:17 refers to him along with his brother John as the "Sons of Thunder." Herod Agrippa beheaded James (Acts 12:2), and historians estimate his death to be around A.D. 41-44.

(2) James, the son of Alphaeus, the Less, probably meaning "the younger," was also one of the 12 Apostles (Matt. 10:3; Mark 3:18; Luke 6:15).

(3) James, the Lord's brother (Matt. 13:55; Mark 6:3; Gal. 1:19), witnessed the first miracle of Jesus at Cana of Galilee (John 2:12). He could be James, the brother of the Lord, as Paul stated, "After that, he was seen of James; then of all the apostles (1 Cor. 15:7).

(4) James, who seems to have remained in Jerusalem where he became a prominent leader in the early church. Read Acts 12:17; 15:13; 21:17-18.

The early church knew James so well that the writer who penned this epistle did not need to identify himself other than "James." After reading several of the N.T. Scriptures and several opinions by Bible scholars, commentators, and historians, I have concluded that we cannot tell from the inspired text with certainty which James penned this book. Thus if God did not reveal the particular James, then it is not a must for us to know.

Although they are not inspired, early historians, the writings of Bible scholars and commentators are profitable in determining dates, kings, corresponding events, and the authenticity of the Book of James. Writers such as "Clement of Rome" (A.D. 96) cited James in his works (James 2:23, 25; 1:8). Therefore, he was acquainted with the book of James. Another is "Polycarp" (A.D.155), who referred to James and his writings; Gregory of Thaumaturgus (A.D. 250), Dionysius of Alexandra (A.D. 260), Origen and Eusebius cited from James (See Rick Billingsley's commentary—The Book of James, pg. 6). Josephus mentions several events that correspond to the Biblical teachings found in James and thus authenticates his writings as reliable sources of information (Antiquities 20:9.1). Albert Barnes' commentary on James probably gives the most detailed explanation of dates, events, and kings, which sheds light on the canonical authority of this epistle.

The writings of several Bible scholars such as J. B. Mayor, Eusebius, and Lightfoot provide reliable sources of information. More recent scholars like James M. Tolle, Rick Billingsley, Robert Harkrider, and Wilson Adams offer valuable insights as one seeks a deeper understanding of the book of James. I recommend reading these various scholars' comments; however, remember they provide their knowledge of the Epistle of James. Commentators and Bible students, including myself, are not incapable of error. The inspired Scriptures are never wrong. It has been said by many that the Bible is its own best commentary.

Chapter 1

wwwwwwwwwwwwwwwwwwwwwwww**Analysis and Brief Summary**

Vv. 1- 12

Writer and Salutation, temptation in the form of trials, the value of trials, faith tested, and unwavering faith. God is the source of heavenly wisdom when one asks in faith. Various warnings against doublemindedness, an admonishment to the brother of low degree and the rich, enduring temptations and the blessedness of unwavering faith.

Vv. 13-15

God is not the source of temptations, how to recognize the source, allurements to sin, enticement, conceiving of sin, and the results of yielding to lust.

Vv. 16-18

The divine source of all blessings, the word of truth, and the first fruits of his creatures.

Vv. 19-20

Be teachable, swift to hear, slow to speak, slow to wrath, and patience.

Vv. 21-25

Forsaking all evil, seek the truth, meek reception of the truth, and practice the truth.

Vv. 26-27

Vain religion versus pure and undefiled religion.

James 1 is about the essence of true religion and discusses various subjects and topics that will be addressed with timely illustrations in chapters two through five. This admonishment, which was written to the first-century brethren, is also applicable to the believers of the twenty-first century. When a child of God understands these truths and makes application in his/her daily lives, then much edification will be wrought, thus producing a mature faith that God requires of all his saints.

Lesson 1—James 1:1-8

Commentary and Questions

1:1—James, A Servant Of God And The Lord Jesus Christ

The writer of this epistle identifies himself by the name James, which is from the Greek *Iakobos*, the Hebrew Jacob, or the late Latin Jacobus. He was probably named after the great forefather of Israel, indicating he was a Jew both by nationality and religion. James identifies himself only as "a servant of God and of the Lord Jesus Christ." He didn't reveal himself as an Apostle, nor claim any physical relationship to the Lord but simply referred to himself as a servant.

There is no higher honor than being a bondservant of God and Jesus Christ. Bondservant (Gr. *doulous*) means slave or servant (W. E. Vine's Dictionary). James was not a slave by constraint but by choice. Jude also opens his epistle by referring to himself as a servant of Jesus Christ and the brother of James (Jude 1). Paul also referred to himself and Timothy as servants of Jesus Christ (Rom. 1:1; Phil. 1:1); also, in Titus 1:1, he refers to himself as "Paul, a servant of God, and of Jesus Christ." Being "a servant of God and servant of the Lord Jesus Christ" emphasizes the fact that James was a servant of Christ, a Christian. Thus indicating to the Jews who had not yet been converted to Christianity that he was a convert of Jesus Christ while acknowledging being a servant of God. All faithful Christians today should think of themselves as servants of God and Jesus Christ, Who died for them and purchased them with His precious blood regardless of one's office, nationality, rank, or station in life. Read Acts 10:34, 35; Ephesians 6:9.

To The 12 Tribes Which Are Scattered Abroad

The writer of this letter mainly addresses "the 12 tribes which are scattered abroad." The ASV says, "to the twelve tribes which are of the Dispersion." The book of Acts records about 3,000 souls were added (Acts 2:41), about 5,000 believed (Acts 4:4), and also, the number was multiplied (Acts 6:1). In Acts 26:7, Paul referred to the 12 tribes of Israel, probably denoting the whole of God's people. Paul seems to address all Christians as children of Abraham by faith in Christ Jesus (Gal. 3:7-9).

James addressed this letter to a specific group of people: those of the Jerusalem church who were scattered outside of Palestine when they left Jerusalem due to persecution (Acts 8:1). The great persecution of the church at Jerusalem scattered them abroad throughout the regions of Judea and Samaria. Saul "made havock of the church, entering into every house, and haling men and women committed them to prison. Therefore, they that were scattered abroad went everywhere preaching the word" (Acts 8:3, 4). Peter also addressed God's elect in his epistle to those in Pontus, Galatia, Cappadocia, Asia, and Bithynia (1 Peter 1:1).

Christians today in a similar sense are commanded by our Lord to go into all the world and preach the Gospel of Jesus Christ as did these early disciples (Matt. 28:19-20; Mark 16:15-16). In all parts of the earth today, God's elect can be seen carrying the gospel or good news of Jesus Christ, which is according to God's foreknowledge.

Greeting

In his salutation to the dispersed, James addresses the thousands of Jews converted to Christianity. The Greek word for greeting is *chairo*, used as a formula of salutation (W.E. Vines Expository Dictionary). According to translators, the church at Jerusalem used "greeting" as "a formula of salutation."

1:2—My Brethren, Count It All Joy
When Ye Fall Into Divers Temptations

"My brethren" seems to pertain to his beloved spiritual brotherhood of believers. The word "brethren" is used at least 15 times by the writer of this letter.

In James 1:2-12, these converts were to "count it all joy," meaning they were to consider it profitable or beneficial when these unwanted trials, afflictions, or persecutions came upon them. If they could rejoice through their trials, it would be profitable for their faith instead of a temptation. There was the "joy" of knowing one remains faithful to the Lord when working through these difficulties, the joy of knowing one's suffering is approved of God, and the joy of understanding God is working things together for one's good (Rom. 8:28). This joy is an internal, spiritual joy rather than an external joy of life which comes from things such as entertainment, pleasures, or recreation.

Obedient believers in Christ should never consider trials, persecution, and calamities as God's punishment because "all that will live godly in Christ Jesus shall suffer persecution" (2 Tim. 3:12). Christians are to count it profitable while these trials are working patience or steadfastness in their lives (1 Pet. 1:6-7).

There are various forms of afflictions and trials in this life, that when endured, will strengthen one's faith and add godly traits of character. Christians are not exempt from adversities in this life, such as sickness or grieving the death of loved ones, calamities such as floods, hurricanes, or tornadoes, as well as persecutions while they are contending earnestly for the faith. All trials are beneficial to one's faith as one works through these adversities. However, all who "earnestly contend for the faith" (Jude 3) in Christ Jesus will be hated by some other religions. Today we are witnessing Islamic domination worldwide. Their Sharia law instructs them to kill those who oppose it. People who oppose the teaching of Islam are being beheaded, bombed, overrun by large trucks, or killed in various other manners. Christians are called infidels and referred to as devils. Mass killings in schools and public gatherings are sanctioned by those who pledge allegiance to a false religion and a god who is not the Jehovah God of the Bible.

Persecutions of other sorts are experienced by Christians today. Those who support the ungodliness of homosexuality or same-sex marriages bring lawsuits against those who teach the truth. Some of our nation's schools and public courthouses are forbidden to display biblical passages or have prayers which mention the name of God or Jesus Christ. So, Christians today must never forget that God can work all things together for their good (Rom. 8:28). Remember, no Christian is exempt from adversities and divers' temptations (1 Cor. 10:13; 1 Pet. 1:4-7).

According to James 1:2, believers are to regard these things as opportunities to rejoice; even though they are grievous and unpleasant, they are nonetheless valuable to their faith. Never should any Christian consider trials of life as a form of punishment, a type of curse, or a sign of guilt. Suffering as a faithful Christian is God approved.

1:3—Knowing This, That The Trying Of Your Faith Worketh Patience

When one's faith is tested, an obedient believer in Jesus Christ should know it can produce the virtue of patience. In this verse, James uses the term for patience meaning that which grows in "the trying of your faith." Faith grows when one abides or remains faithful under life's most difficult circumstances. Faith that stands the test when these afflictions come upon one will work patience time and time again in the lives of an obedient believer.

Knowing that the trying, testing or proving of one's faith works patience is the reason the writer exhorts the brethren to count it all joy in 1:2. Paul also recognized the value of tribulation when he says, "we glory in tribulations also: knowing that tribulation worketh patience; And patience, experience; and experience, hope" (Rom. 5:3, 4). Knowing this, believers can glory in tribulation and that God has a plan when trials overwhelm them; it will benefit them with steadfastness and confident hope of eternal salvation.

So, when trials come one's way, they should never be looked upon as punishment from God, but one should count them as joy or profitable knowing that God has something in mind to the strengthening of one's faith, thus producing endurance. Trials are valuable and beneficial for Christian maturity today as well as it was to the obedient believers of the early church. Every Christian needs patience and perseverance in his/her daily life. Jesus told His disciples that "he that endureth to the end shall be saved" (Matt. 10:22). Read Colossians 1:9-11.

1:4—But Let Patience Have Her Perfect Work

Allow patience to develop or become the fruit of such trials. Patience under trials or endurance produces important effects in our faithfulness as Christians. As one grows in grace and knowledge, one is not to be opposed to God's instructions by murmuring and complaining or being in rebellion to God's working in the believer. When endured, every trial of faith can strengthen one as a good soldier of the cross. So, when these afflictions, disappointments, or dire circumstances challenge one's faithfulness, always remember enduring them allows "patience" to produce "her" desired effect God has intended. "Perfect work" means it will have the precise, complete, finished results of patience that will make one stronger in character as one perseveres while experiencing life's hardships.

That Ye May Be Perfect And Entire, Wanting Nothing

Patience produced in the lives of Christians will aid them in becoming complete or full-grown, spiritually lacking nothing. James uses "perfect" in the sense of becoming spiritually whole, complete or mature as believers endeavor to live godly in this present world. God said of His servant Job that he was a "man who was perfect and upright, and one that feared God, and eschewed evil" (Job 1:1). James is not talking about one being sinless, but patiently enduring hardships helps bring about spiritual growth. Always remember, patience under trials produces important effects on each soul if believers hold up under stresses and strains while awaiting the coming of the Lord. "Perfect and entire" means nothing lacking in spiritual maturity. Trials, afflictions, and persecutions that individual members of the early church were experiencing, when endured today, will bring about spiritual growth, and one can be "perfect and entire, wanting nothing."

1:5—If Any Of You Lack Wisdom, Let Him Ask Of God

As a believer, one needs to understand the definition of heavenly spiritual wisdom. Wisdom from God is defined in two Greek words, (1) sophia and (2) phronesis. "While sophia is the insight to the true nature of things, phronesis is the ability to discern modes of action with a view to their results" (W.E. Vine's Expository Dictionary of N.T. Words). So, when one understands that trials of life are beneficial, one can discern their benefits as they produce patience and endurance. When one asks God in faith, He will give spiritual insight to the benefits of afflictions.

One must realize when James was writing to the early converts, they couldn't turn to other books of the N.T. because the entire Bible was not complete at that time. Christians today can turn to God's word for knowledge because we have the complete, revealed word of God (2 Tim. 3:16-17). So, James, being possibly one of the first N.T. epistles written, admonishes his readers concerning wisdom. First, one must pray to God for wisdom. One needs wisdom to understand the value of each affliction, and then bring the case before God as one asks for understanding and insight in each situation that tries one's faith.

To rejoice in tribulations, one needs to grow in Christlikeness, and for this, one needs wisdom from above that will enable one to form a true evaluation of life's difficulties from God's point of view. Various trials and afflictions in one's life when seeking wisdom from above will produce an accurate assessment of the result, which will work together for one's good (Rom. 8:28; Heb. 12:3-13). God's faithful saints in every age should be willing to take their burdens to the Lord and ask for His divine guidance (Psa. 25:9; Isa. 37:14-20, 33-36). Paul prayed for wisdom from God when seeking the removal of his "thorn in the flesh." God told Paul that His grace was sufficient and would strengthen him to endure whatever this affliction was (2 Cor. 12:7-10). Perhaps Paul then recognized that God could and would work this trial together for his good rather than removing it.

That Giveth To All Men Liberally, And Upbriadeth Not; And It Shall Be Given Him

Without this wisdom from God, the followers of Jesus Christ then and the Christians of today could eventually falter and be overwhelmed by afflictions that often beset God's elect. Therefore, God gives to all men of faith without holding back, reproaching, rebuking, or treating harshly, anyone who prays for His heavenly gift of wisdom. This promise is absolute to the child of God, who asks with the one stipulation in the following verse.

1:6—But Let Him Ask In Faith, Nothing Wavering

When one asks in faith, one must believe God is all-knowing, and nothing is impossible with Him. One cannot expect to receive this wisdom if one doubts God. Asking in faith is the stipulation: "nothing wavering," or doubting God and His ability to give us this insight to the benefits of afflictions and allowing us to understand the results of these trials of life. Paul speaks of Abraham's faith, "He staggered not at the promise of God through unbelief; but was strong in faith, giving glory to God" (Rom. 4:20). Abraham's faith is the kind of faith James speaks of that wavers not when asking God for wisdom. Read Hebrews 11:6.

For He That Wavereth Is Like A Wave Of The Sea Driven With The Wind And Tossed

James uses an example of a wave of the sea, which he likened unto one whose faith wavers. A faithful believer should never doubt that God can and will act upon a "prayer of faith" (James 5:15). Concerning asking for wisdom from above, James likens one's prayer that waivers between faith and unbelief to the wind driving the wave to the shore, like the surges of the sea. It illustrates a person whose faith is unstable in God while making the requests or doubting God's ability to answer. A wave plunges toward the shore and remains for a moment then fades back into the sea. One's faith is "tossed to and fro, and carried about with every wind of doctrine" (Eph. 4:14). Believers then and Christians today should never doubt that God will answer their prayers nor manifest a doubting faith when approaching God for His divine favor.

1:7—For Let Not That Man Think That He Shall Receive Any Thing Of The Lord

Let the doubting person realize his requests for wisdom will not be received because he doubts the Lord's abilities to answer his petitions. The doubter, one who is unstable in his prayer life or who doubts the power of prayer or God's willingness to answer their prayer, will not "receive anything of the Lord." One's faith must be a stable faith that relies upon, trusts in, and depends upon God to supply all of their needs according to His will. Read 1 Peter 3:12.

1:8—A Dobule Minded Man Is Unstable In All His Ways

A "double-minded" person is one who has two minds. Part of the time, he relies upon God, and other times solely relies upon his understanding, intellect, and ability. James affirms that such a person "is unstable in all his ways." James also addresses a double-minded person in 4:8. Being unsettled in their thinking or wavering in their faith, one is not grounded and settled (v. 6).

A double-minded person is one who is torn between two ideas or attempts to straddle both sides of the fence. One cannot be faithful and unfaithful at the same time. With one mind, he attempts to be faithful, but with the other, he is a partaker of worldliness. Jesus said, "No man can serve two masters: for either he will hate the one, and love the other; or else he will hold to the one, and despise the other. Ye cannot serve God and mammon" (Matt. 6:24). A man must devote himself wholeheartedly to God; otherwise, he will be unsettled or uncertain in all his decisions. Likewise, anyone who has double vision cannot focus on heaven with one eye while focusing on worldliness with his other eye (Matt. 6:22, 23).

Lesson One Review Questions For Discussion (1: 1-8)

Verse 1

1. How does James identify himself? _____

2. To whom does James address this epistle? _____

3. Should Christians today be designated as bondservants of God and Jesus Christ? Why? _____

_____

_____

4. What is our purchase price? _____

Verse 2

5. Identify some trials and explain how they can be temptations to one's faith. ____
_____
_____

6. Are Christians today promised a life that is exempt from trials? _____

7. "Yea, and _____ that will live _____ in Christ Jesus shall _____ persecution (2 Timothy 3:12).

8. List some ways in which Christians suffer in school and on the job as believers did in the first century. _____
_____
_____

9. "There hath no _____ taken you but such as is _____ to man: but God is _____, who will not suffer you to be tempted above that ye are _____; but will with the temptation also make a way to _____, that ye may be able to _____ it" (1 Corinthians 10:13).

10. Give some examples from the Book of Acts of the persecution of the saints. __
_____
_____
_____

Verse 3

11. Define patience. _____
_____

12. Is patience a trait of character we must all add to our faith? _____

13. When our faith is tested and we remain faithful, what can it produce? _____

14. How can tribulation work patience in our lives? _____
_____

15. Discuss Matthew 10:22; Romans 5:3; Acts 14:22; Matthew 5:10-12. What things in your daily life tries your patience? _____
_____
_____

Verse 4

16. How can one let "patience have her perfect work?" _____

_____

17. Why does murmuring and complaining keep one from becoming full-grown or mature in the faith? _____

_____

_____

18. How is practicing patience under trials fitted to produce faithfulness to Christ?

_____

19. How can one develop maturity in their Christian life? _____

_____

_____

Verse 5

20. Define wisdom and explain how can it be obtained. _____

_____

_____

21. Can wisdom from above help us endure until the end of our lives? _____
22. Is God's promise of wisdom affirmative and unequivocal when answering our prayers for wisdom? _____

Verse 6

23. What does James mean when he says praying "in faith?" _____

_____

24. Discuss "wavering" and the sea symbol that James uses in his illustration. ____

_____

_____

25. Does James teach conditional praying? Discuss doubting. _____

_____

_____

Verse 7

26. What does the doubter receive from the Lord? _____
27. Is one deceived in their own heart if they think God will answer a doubting prayer? _____

28. "But without _____ it is impossible to please him: for he that cometh to God must _____ that he is, and that he is a _____ of them that _____ seek him (Hebrews 11:6).

Verse 8

29. Define what it means to be doubleminded. _____

_____

_____

30. Does God require total commitment from His saints? _____

Lesson 2—James 1:9-17

⁙⁙⁙⁙⁙⁙⁙⁙⁙⁙⁙⁙⁙Commentary and Questions

1:9—Let The Brother Of Low Degree Rejoice In That He Is Exalted

The brother of low degree or humble circumstances is one who is not rich or famous but rejoices in the fact that God has exalted him. He depends upon God
with singleness of heart and singleness of purpose, unlike the double-minded man
in the preceding verse. Although a Christian might be poor materially speaking,
he can rejoice because God has exalted him with divine favor, and he holds a high
position in the eyes of the Lord. Even though he is of low degree as far as material
wealth, as a child of God, he is rich in that he has God's approval. A poor brother,
instead of wallowing in self-pity, should rejoice in the fact that he is special in God's
sight because he is rich in faith, a child of God, and an heir of heaven.

1:10—But The Rich, In That He Is Made Low: Because As The Flower Of Grass He Shall Pass Away

James is probably referring to rich believers in this verse rather than the rich
non-Christian (5:1-6). Nowhere do the Scriptures say poverty is inherently good, and wealth is inherently evil. Some of God's choicest saints in the
O.T. were wealthy. Abraham, Job, and David are perfect examples. God blessed them abundantly. However, having inherited or earned gain does not condemn the rich, but their condemnation is when their dependency is upon material riches rather than God. Regardless of how many riches one has in life,
God will judge him according to the use of those riches as a good steward.

James refers to the rich being made low by knowing he is "as the flower of grass"
that will soon pass away. The rich Christian is humbled then because he realizes he
can take nothing with him, and riches are only temporal. He realizes his wealth, as
well as his life on earth, will soon be passing away as does the flower of grass. "For we
brought nothing into this world, and it is certain we can carry nothing out" (1 Tim. 6:7).
"Let your conversation be without covetousness; and be content with such things
as ye have: for he hath said, I will never leave thee, nor forsake thee" (Heb. 13:5).

The wealthy person must always maintain a humble spirit and never trust in his
riches. Should a rich Christian's external circumstances change from a state of
wealth/affluence to poverty often challenges his faith. Any drastic change of situ-

21

ations in life can be devastating to one's faith. Likewise, when a brother of humble circumstances changes to a state of affluence/riches, this can cause him to forget the Lord (Read Proverbs 30:8, 9). Perhaps James remembered our Lord's Sermon on the Mount, where He said, "Blessed are the poor in spirit: for theirs is the kingdom of heaven" (Matt. 5:3).

1:11—For The Sun Is No Sooner Risen With A Burning Heat, But It Withereth The Grass, And The Flower Thereof Falleth, And The Grace Of The Fashion Of It Perisheth: So Also Shall The Rich Man Fade Away In His Ways

James expounds upon the figure from the previous verse. The rich man must understand that there can be no reliance upon the things he possesses, neither his pomp nor splendor, for he soon will fade away as does the flower of grass by the burning sun. The humble rich man recognizes his life is fading, and his riches are temporal like the beauty of the "flower" of grass that soon perishes. Likewise, the rich man will fade away in his ways. "For the living know that they shall die" (Eccl. 9:5).

1:12—Blessed Is The Man That Endureth Temptation: For When He Is Tried, He Shall Receive The Crown Of Life, Which The Lord Hath Promised To Them That Love Him

Both the rich and the poor face peculiar trials in this life and must endure temptation. James continues the thought of the benefits for one's faith when subjected to trials and remaining faithful. It is a possibility that he had in mind the same view as our Lord did when He taught the Sermon on the Mount in Matthew 5:4, 10-12. Jesus also used the word "blessed" in His teaching. James now gives the result or the positive side of remaining faithful when one faces temptations in the form of trials or persecutions and stands firm: "He shall receive the crown of life."

When a faithful Christian prays for wisdom, God gives him insight and understanding to the true nature of afflictions. The result will be that he adds patience to his faith, and thus perseverance. The prayer warrior becomes victorious over sufferings; therefore, "joy" can be manifested when patience and endurance empower him. In the end, the result will be the promised "crown of life."

The "crown of life" is a sign of victory or the award from God to those who have overcome. Paul speaks of the promise to the obedient: "having promise of the life that now is, and of that which is to come" (1 Tim. 4:8). Again, Paul speaks of the "crown of righteousness" the Lord will give to him and to all who love His appearing on that day (2 Tim. 4:8). John also penned to the faithful at Smyrna the words of Jesus: "Be thou faithful unto death, and I will give thee a crown of life" (Rev. 2:10). The term "crown" is mentioned many times throughout the Scriptures. Remember, God is not slack concerning His promises: a crown awaits those who faithfully persevere. Each Christian has a cross to bear, and will receive a crown, the sign of victory "to them that love him." Truly, heaven will be worth it all!

1:13—Let No Man Say When He Is Tempted, I Am Temped Of God

James now changes from external temptations in the form of trials (vv. 2-12) to internal temptations in the form of allurements to sin (vv. 13-16). Every serious Bible student needs to read verses 13-16 to understand the entire process of sin and death.

James first says, "Let no man say when he is tempted" that God is the source of temptation to do evil. Just because God created man, he cannot rightfully say, "I was born that way," or "God is tempting me to sin." The inspired writer is teaching that man cannot blame God for his temptations that lead to sin. It is "when he is tempted" rather than will he be tempted. Inward temptations, in one form or another, will continuously confront everyone as well as a child of God. Peter also admonished God's elect to "abstain from fleshly lusts, which war against the soul" (1 Peter 2:11). Lusts of the flesh are a constant battle for every child of God because Satan is relentless. So never attribute sinful allurements to God because He is not the source of temptation. James puts the blame exactly where it belongs: Satan is the author or the source of all sin, not God. Jesus, our Lord, "was in all points tempted like as we are, yet without sin" (Heb. 4:15). Being tempted is not a sin, but it becomes sin when one yields to sinful temptation.

For God Cannot Be Tempted With Evil, Neither Tempteth He Any Man

God is entirely a Holy Being. He cannot sin, and neither does He tempt anyone to sin. The writer denounces even the thought of one claiming God is the source of temptation to do evil. God, in the purity of His character and holiness, is incapable of being seduced by evil. Because of His exalted nature, God cannot be the author or source of evil to "any man."

1:14—But Every Man Is Tempted, When He Is Drawn Away Of His Own Lust, And Enticed

In verses 14-15, James sets forth the progression of sin in the lives of people in the first century as well as today. The word tempt means "to entice, seduce or lure." Lure implies a drawing into danger or evil through attracting and deceiving. Each person is tempted when "drawn away of one's lust and enticed." James is referring to temptation arising from within, from uncontrolled appetites and evil passions. Jesus explains that what defiles a person is within one's heart. "For from within, out of the heart of men, proceed evil thoughts, adulteries, fornications, murders, Thefts, cov-

23

etousness, wickedness, deceit, lasciviousness, an evil eye, blasphemy, pride, foolishness: All these evil things come from within, and defile the man" (Mark 7:21-23).

Though such temptations do not proceed from God, He approves of the faithful believer whose faith is tested. Paul wrote, "There hath no temptation taken you but such as is common to man: but will with the temptation also make a way to escape, that ye may be able to bear it" (1 Cor. 10:13). Joseph is an example of a godly man who resisted temptation by taking the way of escape that God provided (Gen. 39:7-13).

The Scriptures give us insight into three methods used by Satan or his "modus operandi," meaning a "distinct pattern or method of operation" (Merriam-Webster Dictionary). John reveals Satan's M.O., "For all that is in the world, the lust of the flesh, and the lust of the eyes, and the pride of life, is not of the Father, but is of the world" (1 John 2:16). Everyone needs to be careful not to allow these natural fleshly desires to result in sinful or unrestrained passion by (1) the "lust of the flesh." One must bring these fleshly desires or passions of the body into subjection. (2) The "lust of the eyes" is a result of a person who does not refrain from viewing that which is evil such as pornography, nudity, lascivious acts, or other sinful entertainment; thus, lust conceives in one's heart by what one continually sees. (3) The "pride of life" is the boastful evil desire for power and prestige, to crave honor and pomp.

Never is one to blame God for one's sinful passions and inordinate desires. Such things as drug or alcohol abuse, homosexuality, or lascivious acts are learned behaviors that are of the world. One should never allow lust to conceive in the heart because sin is habitual in nature and will enslave. Man creates lust in his own heart when he falls for Satan's devices or allurements by listening to, viewing, or partaking of that which is sinful. All sin first originates in the heart. Sinful addictions like fornication, adultery, and covetousness are the result of sinful desires which mature in the heart. People often ponder in their minds, what fuels the serial rapists, child molesters, murderers, or homosexuals; the answer from Jesus, James, and John may be conceiving lust in one's heart. Paul said the same thing, "Let not sin therefore reign in your mortal body, that ye should obey it in the lusts thereof" (Romans 6:12). One cannot avoid an evil thought under certain circumstances, but when an evil thought crosses the mind, then, one should remove it immediately and not dwell upon it. There is an old true saying: "You can't keep a bird from lighting on your head, but you can keep it from building a nest there." Removing evil thoughts is the first step to avoiding evil desires, which can develop into sinful actions.

1:15—Then When Lust Hath Concieved, It Bringeth Forth Sin

Being tempted is not a sin because our Lord was tempted in all forms, but yielding to evil temptations is a sin. When lust or unrestrained passion has conceived, it can bring about sin. Yielding to temptation is what Jesus was teaching concerning inward purity when He said in Matthew 5:28, "But I say unto you, that whosoever looketh on a woman to lust after her hath committed adultery with her already in his heart." Notice the words "looketh on…to lust after" and "already in his heart." The point being, sin originates in the heart, the heart approves the sin, and then the physical act is committed. Purify your hearts, and the sinful act itself will not be committed. Paul also warned young Timothy to "flee also youthful lusts" (2 Tim. 2:22). Read 2 Corinthians 7:1; Galatians 5:16-17; Ephesians 2:3; 5:16-17; 1 Timothy 6:11; 1 Peter 2:11.

Examine Satan's M.O. used against Eve in the beginning (Gen. 3:1-6). Read how God's servant David sinned with Bathsheba (2 Sam. 11:2-5). Note the temptations and when lust conceives how it brings forth sin. Satan succeeded with Eve and David but failed against our Lord Jesus (Matt. 4:1-11). Satan uses these three forms today and succeeds as he has since the beginning of time. If Satan's methods have worked since the Garden of Eden, why should he change? I am reminded of Jesus' warning to Peter when He said, "Satan hath desired to have you, that he may sift you as wheat" (Luke 22:31).

And Sin, When It Is Finished, Bringeth Forth Death

When one yields to temptation, it is a sin. "Sin" is the transgression of God's laws and separates one from God. When one does not repent of their sins, it results in eternal separation from God, which stands in contrast to the "crown of life" (1:12). It behooves each Christian to learn Satan's devices and "Abstain from all appearance of evil" (1 Thess. 5:22). Satan is portrayed "as a roaring lion, walketh about, seeking whom he may devour" (1 Peter 5:8). If overtaken by worldly temptations, one should never forget the Advocate with the Father, Jesus Christ the Righteous, who can intercede on a Christian's behalf. He knows all about Satan's devices concerning temptations because He was tempted in all forms as all people are, yet He was without sin. One must always have a humble spirit by going to God in prayer, confessing all sins, and repenting so one can enjoy this continual cleansing from sin (1 John 1:7-10).

Sin then is brought about through a process. Conceiving sin in the heart could result in one committing that sin, thus bringing about separation from God. Anyone who indulges in a sinful thought or a corrupt desire should think in terms of it causing spiritual separation from God and its end result of eternal death. One should rid the mind of every sinful thought and desire when confronted with allurements that will bring about transgression of God's law. To eliminate unwanted thoughts, one can always pray, quote Scripture, or sing praises unto the Lord when evil thoughts cross the mind. "Resist the devil, and he will flee from you" (James 4:7).

1:16—Do Not Err, My Beloved Brethren

"Be not deceived, my beloved brethren" (ASV) was probably said in connection to those readers who had misguided opinions concerning temptations of life, as is stated in verse 13. James warns the brethren not to be deceived by ascribing to God the blame for sin. Fleshly, inherent desires have a purpose in one's life, but one should never forget God also has a prescribed order for the fulfillment of these natural desires. Paul instructs young Timothy: "Flee also youth lusts" (2 Tim. 2:22). Peter says to "abstain from fleshly lusts, which war against the soul" (1 Peter 2:11).

Every child of God, young or old, faces this spiritual warfare of fighting temptations. "Fight the good fight of faith," as Paul tells Timothy (1 Tim. 6:12). "The carnal mind is enmity against God" (Rom. 8:7). "Present your bodies a living sacrifice, holy, acceptable unto God, which is your reasonable service. And be not conformed to this world" (Rom. 12:1-2). There is the battle of self where one must refuse the allurements to sin and fight the good fight of faith, always choosing the paths of righteousness by bringing one's thoughts and mind in subjection to the perfect will of God. Every Christian fights the spiritual warfare between the flesh and the Spirit (Gal. 5:17). The Bible lists a catalog of sins of which Christians must never be partakers (Gal. 5:19-21). The apostle Paul instructs faithful brethren to focus their thinking on these things instead: "Finally, brethren, whatsoever things are true, whatsoever things are honest, whatsoever things are just, whatsoever things are pure, whatsoever things are lovely, whatsoever things are of good report; if there be any virtue, and if there be any praise, think on these things" (Phil. 4:8). In other words, stay focused on these things, "and the God of peace shall be with you" (Phil. 4:9). The inspired wise man of God says in Proverbs 23:7, "For as he thinketh in his heart, so is he." David, a man after God's own heart, said, "Thy word have I hid in mine heart, that I might not sin against thee" (Psa. 119:11). The point to these Scriptures is to choose the right things to think about, and then focus on them. If you suddenly begin to think about evil things, stop immediately and refocus.

1:17—Every Good Gift And Every Perfect Gift Is From Above

In 1:16-17, James tells his beloved brethren not to err in their thinking. God is not the source of temptations. The Lord is never the source of evil, but rather only goodness proceeds from God.

The difference between a "good gift" and a "perfect gift" may be difficult for a person to explain or to understand correctly. The Bible describes some things in life as good but calls some things perfect. Some things are both good and perfect. James says gifts from God are both good and perfect. Certain things are good but are lacking in some point and thus not perfect. Probably the meaning here is that all good gifts and perfect gifts are from above, thus meaning from God.

The Greek word for good is *agathos*, which means it is beneficial in its effect. The Greek word for perfect is *teleios* meaning complete, finished (W.E. Vine's Dictionary). Some often look at material blessings from God as being "good" meaning beneficial or necessary, while spiritual blessings that pertain to man's salvation are perfect (Psa. 19:7-11). God has given us everything we need when overcoming all temptations. God is the source Who gives only that which is good and never evil. One can trace everything good thing on earth to God. Evil has another origin.

And Cometh Down From The Father Of Lights, With Whom Is No Variableness, Neither Shadow Of Turning

God is the creator of all light. Jesus, our Lord, is also spoken of as "the light of the world." The source or the fountain of every blessing comes from above. God created the greater light to rule the day and the lesser light to rule the night. These lights vary in the amount of light they give off. The sun comes up to light the day and then fades away at night. The moon and the stars give light at night, but at daybreak, their light fades away. The writer alludes to these emblems of light in comparison to God's giving every good and perfect gift, which never varies. "God is light, and in Him is no darkness at all" (1 John 1:5). God is the source of all moral light and purity and doesn't change or leave a "shadow of turning." Take, for example, the illustration of a match: when it is lit and held near a white wall, it will leave no shadow. This illustration should remind one of our God, Who never changes or manifests a shadow of turning. God is the source of all blessings, both material and spiritual. In the Scriptures, light is the emblem of purity, knowledge, and happiness. In this way, Jesus is portrayed as "the light of the world," shinning in a world of darkness. Light dispels darkness as Jesus enables man to see the light and walk in the paths of God's righteousness.

In 1897, N.L. Caton penned these words concerning no variableness, neither shadow of turning: "The fountain of the light which reaches this earth is the sun. Its rays do not always reach us. They are turned aside by intervening clouds. Not so with the Father of lights. With Him, there is no change, no turning. He is unchangeable. He gives good gifts, and none other. He does not approach us, and then retire. He is always near, all in all. It is simply blasphemous, as well as absurd, to entertain the suggestion of his being the author of influences inciting to evil."

Lesson Two Review Questions For Discussion (1: 9-17)

Verse 9

1. How can the brother of low degree find reason to rejoice? _____

_____

2. List some of the unsearchable riches of Christ which cause a Christian to rejoice today (Eph. 3:8). _____

_____

Verse 10

3. How does James' illustration of the flower of grass show the rich is made low?

_____

_____

4. Why are there dangers of riches and poverty (Proverbs 30: 8, 9)? _____

_____

_____

Verse 11
5. In what ways are the riches of the rich fading away? _____

_____

6. Since one can't take their riches with them beyond the grave, what will remain at the resurrection (Luke 14: 13-14)? _____

_____

Verse 12
7. Define the word crown. _____

_____

8. What must one do to receive the "crown of life?" _____

_____

Verse 13
9. Why can no one blame God when they are tempted? _____

_____

_____

10. How can one know that it is not a sin to be tempted? _____

_____

Verse 14
11. Define the word lust. _____

_____

12. What is Satan's M.O. when it comes to lust (1 John 2:16)? _____

_____

13. What can one learn from the Lord's success when facing the temptations of the devil (Matt. 4), unlike the failure of Eve and David? _____

_____

_____

Verse 15

14. What is the process of sin that will lead to separation from God? _____
_____
_____

Verse 16

15. Considering the context, explain what James means when he says, "Do not err,
my beloved brethren." _____
_____

Verse 17

16. How are God's gifts both good and perfect? _____
_____

17. Is God ever the source of evil? _____

Lesson 3—James 1:18-25

Commentary and Questions

1:18—Of His Own Will Begat He Us With The Word Of Truth

It is through God's purpose and planning that He "begat" or brought us forth to be His children through Jesus Christ, our Lord. Redemption is traced to God's "own will" as the source. We are begotten of God "with the word of truth." The term "word" is found several times in verses 18-25 and refers to the Scriptures or the Word of God by which we are saved.

John refers to the "Word" in John 1:13, 14, as being the One who took upon Himself the form of flesh and dwelt among us as the only begotten of the Father. The point here is "the word of truth" brings forth life where sin brings forth death (v. 15). Jesus proclaimed, "I am the way, the truth, and the life" (John 14:6). Of His own will, God, prompted by His love, purposed and planned our salvation through Jesus Christ, which is revealed by the "word of truth." God had no outside source prompting Him to draw salvation's plan. When the seed (Luke 8:11), which is "the word of truth," becomes implanted or engrafted (James 1:21) in good and honest hearts, it will "begat" or bring forth life. God purposed, planned, and predestinated this before the foundation of the world (Eph. 1:4, 5).

That We Should Be A Kind Of Firstfruits Of His Creatures

Those who have been begotten by the Gospel are the "firstfruits" of a bountiful harvest. In Leviticus 23:10, there is an indication of a harvest to come that belonged to God. Those Jewish brethren, servants of the Lord Jesus Christ that were scattered abroad, had the honor of being referred to as the "firstfruits of his creatures." The Gospel was preached to the Jew first, and then to the Greek or Gentile (Rom. 1:16; 2:9,10; Gal. 3:27-28). These obedient believers who obeyed the Gospel of Jesus Christ were the first group of converts. After the Gospel spread to Samaria and the uttermost parts of the earth, a greater group would follow. James may be referring to all who are begotten by the "word of truth" (v. 18.) He addresses those who had obeyed the Gospel of Jesus Christ and were continuing in the apostles' doctrine (Acts 2:38, 47) with the high honor of being referred to as the "firstfruits" of the Gospel.

31

1:19—Wherefore, My Beloved Brethren,
Let Every Man Be Swift To Hear, Slow To Speak, Slow To Wrath

"Wherefore" means to consider what James is about to say in view of what was previously stated. Previously James stated that God tempts no man to do evil (v. 13), is only the source of good not evil (v. 17), has begotten believers by the word of truth, and conferred upon them the honor of being the firstfruits of His creation (v. 18). Because of these facts, all Christians have the responsibility to receive with meekness the engrafted word which is able to save their souls. The reception of truth (vv. 19-21) demands God's firstfruit of His creatures to be swift to hear, slow to speak, and slow to wrath.

"Swift to hear" means Christians must be good listeners or quick to listen, always attentive to God's instructions of the truth by which they are begotten. The readiness to listen to God's counsel in all matters pertaining to the faith is crucial as one grows in grace and knowledge. This willingness to listen not only applies to when one obeys the Gospel of Jesus Christ but also that which relates to one's duties as an obedient believer. Hearing the word of God strengthens one's faith and one must always be willing to be guided by what the Scriptures reveal. "So then faith cometh by hearing, and hearing by the word of God" (Rom. 10:17). Also, one of the major problems among church members today is the lack of communication. One must practice being a good listener to eliminate a lot of internal problems among brethren.

Let us understand this is a command of God that one be "slow to speak." Often people are just the opposite. Since God "begat" the obedient believers by the word of truth, the need to be "slow to speak" could either refer to those who are quick to blame God for their sins (v. 14) or to those who speak too hastily in their communication with others. Christians today often regret being too quick to speak rather than being good listeners. Someone once asked a man why he met the reproaches of others with a profound silence. He replied, "I have sometimes had occasion to regret that I have spoken, never that I was silent" (Barnes Notes, James 1:19, p. 29). Peter is an example of one who seemingly was quick to speak, but after learning this truth said, "For he that will love life, and see good days, let him refrain his tongue from evil, and his lips that they speak no guile" (1 Peter 3:10). The wise man writes, "Be not rash with thy mouth, and let not thine heart be hasty to utter any thing before God" (Eccl. 5:2). James will go into great detail in Chapter 3 concerning the sins of the tongue.

"Slow to wrath" means not easily angered; this is one who is gentle, peaceable, easily entreated, kind and tenderhearted. As the elect of God today, Christians are to govern or restrain their temper. The inspired, wise man of God instructs, "He that is slow to anger is better than the mighty; and he that ruleth his spirit than he that taketh a city" (Prov. 16:32). "He that is slow to wrath is of great understanding: but he that is hasty of spirit exalteth folly" (Prov. 14:29). In Ephesians 4:31, Paul writes to Christians to put away the following: bitterness meaning bitter hatred, wrath meaning hot anger, anger meaning a natural impulse that can be turned into wrath, clamour meaning a tumult of controversy or outcry, and evil speaking meaning defaming someone's character. All these were to be put away along with malice, which involves a vicious character associated with evil. Paul commanded these believers to be "kind one to another, tenderhearted, forgiving one another, even as God for Christ's sake hath forgiven you" (Eph. 4:32). The person who is easily angered becomes unteachable because he becomes inflamed when others disagree with him or attempt to teach him the truth.

1:20—For The Wrath Of Man Worketh Not The Righteousness Of God

"Wrath" does not produce "the righteousnes," which God requires in the life of an obedient believer. Wrath or hot anger is the opposite of "speaking the truth in love" (Eph. 4:15). When anger, wrath, clamor and railing abound in one's heart, it hinders the cause of Christ. One whose speech and actions are characterized by a spirit of wrath or argumentative abusive behavior is not a defender of the Gospel but is an offender and never sure of doing that which is right in God's sight. A Christian can justify anger only if it is a natural emotion that does not cause one to sin (Eph. 4:26, 27, 31-32). Paul writes to the saints and faithful brethren at Colosse that all should walk in wisdom by their manner of speech when he said, "Let your speech be always with grace, seasoned with salt, that ye may know how ye ought to answer every man" (Col. 4:6). Truly, man's wrath does not work "the righteousness of God." Read Ecclesiastes 7:9.

1:21—Wherefore Lay Apart All Filthiness And Superfluity Of Naughtiness

Because God has begotten us with the word of truth, we are to lay aside or entirely discard all impurity that arises from the lusts of the flesh that James speaks about in the previous verses. Since God has begotten us for His service, we are not to allow bitterness, anger, and wrath to reign in our hearts. We are to put away all "filthiness," which is a course of conduct that is evil and offensive to God. Sin is a violation of God's law, and we are to put it away or avoid anything that will characterize "filthiness." "Superfluity of naughtiness" is that which abounds in our lives that is evil to the highest degree or the overflowing of anything that is not according to the perfect will of God. When our minds become corrupt with sensuality or an overflowing of wicked desires, we will not be subject to fulfilling God's righteousness. Jesus said, "Blessed are the pure in heart: for they shall see God" (Matt. 5:8).

And Receive With Meekness The Engrafted Word, Which Is Able To Save Your Souls

"Meekness," as James uses it here, refers to the inward exercise of the heart towards God, one who opens his heart and mind to God's instructions. A meek person is one that hears God's instruction and then humbly receives the good word of God by welcoming the knowledge of God in their heart. When God's word is engrafted or implanted in the heart, it will result in the salvation of one's soul. The engrafted word saves, but only when one obeys it! James seems to introduce this thought as he elaborates in his following admonishment in the next verse and the remainder of this epistle. Seemingly James uses chapter 1 as an introduction of what he will discuss and illustrate in the remaining four chapters of this epistle.

1:22—But Be Ye Doers Of The Word, And Not Hearers Only, Deceiving Your Own Selves

The person who is a hearer of the word only, and not a doer of what the word says, deceives himself as if his hearing only is what pleases God. At the conclusion of His Sermon on the Mount, our Lord Jesus settled this matter once and for all. Our Lord and Master said, "Therefore whosoever heareth these sayings of mine, and doeth them, I will liken him unto a wise man, which built his house upon a rock" (Matt. 7:24). The hearer only was likened unto a foolish man who built upon the sand (Matt.7:26). The house of the wise man stood firm while the foolish man's work fell because it lacked a solid foundation. So, it is with anyone who hears the word and is not a doer. Obeying the gospel is more than listening to the word proclaimed. Obedience requires the application of the truth learned. People can sit in the pew and listen to sound gospel preaching and teaching, but unless they make the proper application, what influence will it have on their lives that is pleasing to God? It goes through one ear and out the other.

1:23-24—For If Any Be A Hearer Of The Word, And Not A Doer, He Is Like Unto A Man Beholding His Natural Face In A Glass: For He Beholdeth Himself, And Goeth His Way, And Straightway Forgetteth What Manner Of Man He Was

James illustrates the hearer only and not a doer to a person who bends forward, looks in a mirror, and observes a blemish of some sort on the face. After beholding the image, the person turns around and does nothing about the blemish. James illustrates the hearer only as one who hears the good word of God, realizes their blemishes or defects as God sees them, and then turns away without correcting the imperfection. When people hear the good word of God, it reveals their shortcomings, defects, and blemishes in their moral character like a mirror reflects their actual physical appearance. As a mirror truthfully reflects one's natural face, so the word of God reflects one's actual spiritual state that reveals one's blemished soul. Many times, it has been said to gospel preachers as brethren exit the assembly, "I really needed to hear that message from God's word. It seems as if you were speaking directly to me." How foolish it is for us as Christians to recognize our imperfections and then walk away, failing to make the necessary changes!

1:25—But Whoso Looketh Into The Perfect Law Of Liberty, And Contineth Therein, He Being Not A Forgetful Hearer, But A Doer Of The Work, This Man Shall Be Blessed In His Deed

"Looketh" elaborates upon what it means to behold, by stooping down, bending forward or turning sideways and looking as closely as possible. One gets a closer examination of oneself while observing what one sees when looking "into the perfect law of liberty," which will reflect one's true appearance as God sees. James refers to the Scriptures in this verse as the "perfect law of liberty." Perfect law refers to God's law as a perfect standard of conduct (2 Tim. 3:16-17; 2 Peter 1:3). The psalmist refers to the law of the Lord as perfect or lacking nothing (Psa. 19:7-11). Jesus teaches us that it will be the standard of judgment on that day (John 12:48).

"Law of liberty" could mean that which frees people from sinful passions and lusts, as mentioned in the previous verses. There is also the possibility that "liberty" here may be understood as freedom from Moses' law as far as eating certain meats, observing holy days, Sabbath days, and keeping sacramental aspects of the Old Law. No doubt, James' fellow Jewish brethren could relate to this description of God's law as "perfect." Read Paul's teaching in Colossians 2:14-17 and other companion verses which show this perfection of the Gospel's saving power (law of liberty) versus the law of Moses (Gal. 3:21; Heb. 7:19; and Heb. 10:1-18).

When one looks in the mirror of God's word, one can see the blemishes in one's life, but one must not turn away before correcting those errors or faults. One must always be willing to remove those blemishes by obedience to the teachings of the "perfect law of liberty," which is God's perfect system for man's salvation. The Christian life is a continual growing process of becoming more and more like the Master Who is perfect in character. One can be perfect in the sense of being free from guilt and the power and punishment of sin so one can enjoy the continuous cleansing of the blood of Jesus Christ (1 John 1:7).

James M. Tolle expresses in his writings, "Only the Christian who obeys God from a loving heart and a clear conscience will find life's greatest blessedness, the true happiness that is inherit in following Christ. See John 8:31; 10:10; 1 Peter 3:9-12." Possibly James remembered God's instructions to the children of Israel: "Only take heed to thyself, and keep thy soul diligently, lest thou forget the things which thine eyes have seen, and lest they depart from thy heart all the days of thy life..." (Deut. 4:9). A faithful believer in Christ will not forget what he hears regarding God's will but will become a doer in his zeal for good works. Read Titus 1:16.

Lesson Three Review Questions For Discussion (1:18-25)

Verse 18

1. Define the word "begat." _____

James ——————————————————————————————————

2. Who "begat" us and by what means? _____

_____

3. In the book of Acts, how were Christians brought forth or converted? ____

_____

_____

Verse 19
4. What does it mean to be:
   a. "swift to hear" _____

   _____

   b. "slow to speak" _____

   _____

   c. "slow to wrath" _____

   _____

5. What does lacking these traits of character often fuel? _____

_____

Verse 20
6. When accomplishing God's righteousness, why is it important to avoid wrath
   and anger? _____

   _____

7. Define wrath. _____

   _____

8. What is the meaning of "seasoned with salt" in one's manner of speech as Paul
   used it in Colossians 4:6? _____

   _____

Verse 21
9. Why should one lay aside all "filthiness" and evil conduct? _____

_____

_____

10. How does Jesus' teaching of the "pure in heart" relate to what James is teach-
    ing? _____

    _____

11. When we receive with meekness the implanted or engrafted word, what will be
    the result? _____

Verse 22

12. What does it mean to be a "doer of the word?" _____

_____

13. How can a person who is a hearer and not a doer deceive himself in thinking he is pleasing to God? _____

_____

Verse 23-24

14. Give an example of how one could be guilty of looking into the mirror of God's word, seeing a blemish, and then going away forgetting what manner of person they are, thus failing to correct the flaw. _____

_____

Verse 25

15. Who is the person who will be blessed of God in his deeds? _____

_____

16. How does the word perfect used by Paul in 2 Timothy 3:16-17 relate to the word perfect used by James. _____

_____

_____

Lesson 4—James 1:26-27; 2:1-7

~~~~~~~~~~~~~~~~~~~~~~~~~~~Commentary and Questions

1:26—If Any Man Among You Seem To Be Religious, And Bridleth Not His Tongue

"If any man among you" refers to any believer professing to be a devout person while not restraining their tongue. Failing to control their speech overrides other evidence of this person being righteous. One of the characteristics of a godly person is one who restricts his tongue. Being slow to speak and bridling the tongue is an attribute of a religious person who is serious about serving God.

Most mature people know, especially those of James's day, what it means to bridle a mule or horse. They put a bridle on a horse with bits in its mouth to bring the animal into submission (3:3). Thus, by restraining the tongue or selecting the proper words, they can bring their whole bodies into subjection (3:6). As will be seen in James 3:1-12, every sin committed involves the tongue. In chapter 3, James will be discussing the sins of an unbridled tongue, which, in my opinion, is the most concise teaching I have ever studied concerning the sins of the tongue. James seems to introduce the thought here in this verse as being a part of practicing pure Christianity.

An unbridled tongue shows the opposite of one professing godliness. James has just revealed in the preceding verses the right attitude towards receiving the word of truth but now alludes to how one can demonstrate being a doer of the word rather than just a hearer. One of the first ways Christians prove they are children of God is by putting a leash on the tongue by being very careful to restrict what is said to others. God requires more than going to the assembly of the church to be accounted faithful. One must practice pure Christianity in one's everyday words.

But Deceiveth His Own Heart, This Man's Religion Is Vain.

One who thinks he is religious as God would have him to be but fails to watch what he says to others has deceived himself into thinking God approves his religion. This man's religion is vain, worthless, or void if he daily wags his tongue without carefully choosing his words. Jesus said, "But I say unto you, that every idle word that men shall speak, they shall give account thereof in the day of Judgement. For by thy words thou shalt be justified, and by thy words thou shalt be condemned" (Matt. 12:36-37). How sad to stand before the judgement seat of Christ and be condemned because of the misuse of the tongue!

1:27—Pure Religion And Undefiled
Before God And The Father Is This

James now introduces what most Bible scholars refer to as the theme or subject of this entire epistle. He instructs the individual believer to practice pure and undefiled religion before God the Father. Pure and undefiled are two adjectives describing one's religion that meets God's approval.

"Pure" is from the Greek word *katharos* meaning one is "pure, as being cleansed" by the blood of Jesus (Matt. 26:28). "Undefiled" is from the Greek word *amiantos* meaning "free from contamination" (W.E. Vines Dictionary). A religious person who is not self-seeking and manifests love and mercy towards others is like God the Father. He is holy, generous, and merciful to others. When one lives according to God's will, one's religion will be pure and undefiled, which is the kind of religion that meets the approval of God and is genuine in His sight.

The words "religion" and "religious" appear a half dozen times or so in the N.T. The word religion in everyday language, basically means what one professes, believes, lives, worships, obeys, and acts upon. One's worship can be scriptural (John 4:24), in vain (Matt. 15:9), or in ignorance (Acts 17:23).

God observes one's daily manner of life. All disciples of Christ must prove their lives to be religious before God by bridling or restraining the tongue, displaying proper benevolence to his fellowman, and displaying the appropriate conduct of godly living in one's daily life. Christians today must realize God views all manners of their lives when it comes to purity, holiness, and benevolence.

To Visit The Fatherless And Widows In Their Affliction

Now, James gives a perfect example of a truly religious person displaying pure and undefiled religion before God. The word "visit" means to go see, look upon in order to help, to care for, or to show a personal interest in someone. The Greek word *episkeptomia* is more than a casual visit but means to look upon with the idea of benefiting or helping the fatherless and widows in their afflictions.

"Fatherless" is from the Greek word *orphanos*, properly, an orphan, and is translated "fatherless" in James 1:27. "Widow" is from the Greek word *chera*, lit., a woman a widow (see W.E. Vine's Dictionary). The word widow is found numerous times in the Scriptures, which denotes one whose husband is deceased. It is my understanding that James is encouraging each believer as an individual to aid these two groups when they are destitute and unable to help themselves.

Caring for involves any help one can provide in the lives of the afflicted and suffering. James commands the individual believer, "As we have therefore opportunity, let us do good unto all men, especially unto them who are of the household of faith" (Gal. 6:10). All Christians today who avoid personal contact and acts of benevolence in the lives of the suffering are not practicing pure religion of which James speaks (1:27). Those individual believers who have the means and opportunity to help the destitute, by doing so, are fulfilling this command. Barnes Notes elaborates, "This is the instance or specimen of what true religion will do, showing that it will lead to a life of practical benevolence." He also states, "This has always been regarded as an essential thing in true religion," and then he cites Psalms 68:5.

The O.T. is filled with many passages instructing people who are to imitate God, Who is benevolent. An individual who imitates God will be a benevolent person who is always ready to help those who cannot help themselves. This example of the "fatherless" and "widows" are two instances of people who, in their time of affliction, need to be visited and looked upon with the idea of helping. God approves of the benevolent person who has an eye to recognize and a loving heart that is ready to aid the helpless when one has the ability and opportunity. Jesus taught His disciples to give "alms" or do alms-deeds (Matt. 6:1-4). There are also other passages in the N.T. which instruct God's people to show forth mercy, love, and pity on the poor. It behooves each Christian today to examine themselves by asking, "Am I practicing pure religion before God?"

Just last Lord's day where I worship, I noticed three more young babies of a different race and only a few weeks old that have been adopted by one faithful, benevolent Christian couple. Others in the same congregation have adopted and are opening their homes to children who are either orphans or unwanted children who need people to open their hearts and home. Thus these Christians are showing forth love and godly benevolence. They are practicing pure religion by this personal involvement of aiding the destitute who cannot help themselves.

And To Keep Himself Unspotted From The World

The first part of this verse (1:27) teaches if a man is benevolent, he is like God. The latter part of the verse teaches if a man is unspotted by the world, he is like God in so much as he is holy or untarnished by sin. God sees man's benevolent acts, and also God observes man's pure manner of life. See comments on James 1:14 concerning "lust" and keeping oneself from these worldly lusts. John says in 1 John 2:15, "Love not the world, neither the things that are in the world. If any man love the world, the love of the Father is not in him." James states, "Know ye not that the friendship of the world is enmity with God?" (4:4). Paul says in Romans 12:1-2, "I beseech you therefore, brethren, by the mercies of God, that ye present your bodies a living sacrifice, holy, acceptable unto God, which is your reasonable service. And be not conformed to this world: but be ye transformed by the renewing of your mind, that ye may prove what is that good, and acceptable, and perfect will of God."

Chapter 2

Analysis and Brief Summary

Vv. 1-7

James addresses the issue of showing partiality and the sin of partiality when one despises the poor by having respect of persons. Faith in Christ recognizes no such distinctions. God does not approve of any such distinctions in the assembly of the church or among brethren.

Vv. 8-13

Fulfilling the royal law is mandated rather than showing partiality or prejudices that are sinful. Mercy rejoices against judgment. God does not extend mercy to one who has not shown mercy. Speak and act as one who will be judged by the law of liberty.

Vv. 14-26

Faith apart from works is dead being alone. Faith is dead if it is without good deeds. Abraham and Rahab, the harlot, are two Biblical examples of faith and works.

Lesson 4 (cont.)—James 1:26-27; 2:1-7

~~~~~~~~~~~~~~~~~~~~~~~~~ Commentary and Questions

2:1—My Brethren, Have Not The Faith Of Our Lord Jesus Christ, The Lord Of Glory, With Respect Of Persons

The ASV reads, "My brethren, hold not the faith of our Lord Jesus Christ, the Lord of glory, with respect of persons." Holding or maintaining the faith of our Lord Jesus Christ with partiality or distinctions is forbidden by the Lord of glory. Today, those who practice true Christianity will not show partiality or favoritism because of one's wealth, rank, education, or race.

Christianity is a religion that displays love, compassion, and concern for the welfare of everyone who belongs to Christ. He died for all regardless of one's background or status in life. The saints that were scattered abroad were instructed not to show partiality among those who maintain "the Faith." This type of distinction among brethren is what James is condemning.

The Jews of the first century would often divide themselves into groups such as Pharisees, Sadducees, Essenes, and Zealots. Many Jewish believers in the early church continued this type of attitude displaying favoritism to the elite. People may play favorites, but God does not and forbids others to do so. So, Christians of the twenty-first century can also understand that God does not approve of partiality, favoritism, or "respect of persons" by displaying more honor to some than others.

The Law of Moses condemned showing respect of persons. Moses said, "And I charged your judges at that time, saying, Hear the causes between your brethren, and judge righteously between every man and his brother, and the stranger that is with him. Ye shall not respect persons in judgment; but ye shall hear the small as well as the great" (Deut. 1:16, 17). The Jews didn't always obey this command. We also see this type of attitude in the early church, and it may even exist in the twenty-first-century congregations of the Lord's church.

The text uses the Greek word *prosopolempsia* which "denotes respect of persons, partiality, the fault of one who, when responsible to give judgement, has respect to the position, rank, popularity, or circumstances of men, instead of their intrinsic conditions, preferring the rich and powerful to those who are not so, Rom. 2:11; Eph. 6:9; Col. 3:25; James 2:1" (W.E. Vines Dictionary of N.T. Words). One who professes to be in Christ should treat others as equals. There are no big I's and little you's in the Lord's church. Prejudice, partiality, and showing "respect of persons" have no place in the body of Christ.

2:2—For If There Come Unto Your Assembly A Man With A Gold Ring, In Goodly Apparel, And There Come In Also A Poor Man In Vile Raiment

James now illustrates partiality by giving two examples of people who might appear in the assembly. One enters the assembly appearing to be rich, displaying a gold ring, a common ornament of the rich, "in goodly apparel" or fancy attire. The other enters the assembly appearing to be poor, dressed "in vile raiment," denoting poverty. Like some Christians today, the Jews often divided themselves into groups similar to clicks. Matthew 23:6 mentions the scribes and Pharisees who loved "the chief seats in the synagogues." They often separated themselves from others and, in some cases, rejected others because of religious beliefs. These groups were common in the days of our Lord (see Luke 14:7-9; Luke 20:46-47).

2:3—And Ye Have Respect To Him That Weareth The Gay Clothing, And Say Unto Him, Sit Thou Here In A Good Place; And Say To The Poor, Stand Thou There, Or Sit Here Under My Footstool

The ASV reads, "And ye have regard to him that weareth the fine clothing." If you have respect for the one dressed in fine or fancy clothing, yet the one in vile clothing is asked to stand over there against the wall or sit on the floor, then you have shown the respect of persons and thus dishonored the poor for whom the Lord died. In the church today, if Christians greet a visitor who is dressed in fancy clothing and fail to show the same honor by welcoming the poor or those wearing ordinary attire, then they have shown respect of persons. One who practices true Christianity before God will not make a distinction in greeting visitors to the assembly. When Christians give the rich special places to sit and the disrespect the poor, God is displeased with such partiality.

2:4—Are Ye Not Then Partial In Yourselves, And Are Become Judges Of Evil Thoughts

The temptation is to judge according to appearance and give special attention to the one dressed in fine clothing. Read what some of the Scriptures in the O.T. and the N.T. have to say about judging according to appearance (1 Sam. 16:7; 2 Cor. 5:12; 10:7). Jesus said in John 7:24, "Judge not according to the appearance, but judge righteous judgment." When followers of Jesus Christ are partial to the rich, are they not valuing the person or soul of the rich above that of the poor? (See comments on James 1:10).

In showing partiality, a person becomes like the evil judges of Jesus' day who judged according to appearance. Some could have evil motives for seeking the favor of the rich. One should warmly welcome the rich and extend the same treatment to the poor. When one shows partiality and becomes judges of evil thoughts, Rick Billingsley writes in his commentary on James, "James is not teaching that to be wealthy is sinful. The rich man who came to the same church services as the poor man was not condemned because of his affluence. The usher committed the sin of giving greater respect to the rich man. James draws attention to the fact that the reason most people commit the sin of respect of persons is that they have an erroneous sense of values. This is made clear in verses 3 and 4. Prejudicial actions are the symptoms of a much deeper problem, evil thinking. There is an evil motive behind being prejudiced. This motive can be many things" (p. 25).

Some had taken upon themselves the role of judges (Matt. 7:1-2). Some of the converts in the early church often showed favoritism to the wealthy. Neither the rich nor the poor were condemned for coming into the assembly. All classes and races of people needed salvation, but God condemned the prejudicial thinking of some who had a false sense of the value concerning souls. They were "judges" in the sense of making distinctions because of external appearances.

Even today, in some congregations of Christians who are so high-minded and stiffed-necked, judging people by appearance rather than viewing them as people who are needing salvation takes place. Greeting strangers in a congregation of God's people and making all feel a warm welcome is the first step to being soul winners. When Christians learn the value of a soul, they will show forth the same hospitality to all visitors. A soul winner always practices hospitality with a warm welcome. Christians should examine themselves as to whether or not they are God approved in this matter.

2:5—Hearken, My Beloved Brethren, Hath Not God Chosen The Poor Of This World Rich In Faith, And Heirs Of The Kingdom Which He Hath Promised To Them That Love Him

James is about to ask several questions in the next few verses to provoke their thoughts and remind them of things most likely they already knew as to why they shouldn't show favoritism. "Harken my beloved brethren" means for his brethren to listen closely to his words of admonition. Then he asks a thought-provoking question: "Hath not God chosen the poor of this world rich in faith, and heirs of the kingdom which he hath promised to them that love him?" Disrespecting the poor because of their appearance is not consistent with the gospel call.

He reminds them of God's provisions for the poor of this world, who are "rich in faith." They will be "heirs of the kingdom," which God has promised to all men, rich or poor, who fear Him. (Read 1 Peter 1:1-9). The poor were more likely to receive by faith the gospel message than the wealthy. "Not many wise men after the flesh, not many mighty, and not many noble, are called" (1 Cor. 1:26). The common man is more likely to hear the Lord as Mark records, "the common people heard him gladly" (Mark 12:37) because they did not trust in the abundance of uncertain riches. The rich man with his riches would be more likely to reject the truth because of his dependency upon material riches rather than dependency upon God. God promised that all who loved Him would inherit the kingdom, an excellent reason not to despise the poor as some had done in these passages.

2:6—But Ye Have Despised The Poor

By looking upon the poor with contempt (2:3), they had despised, dishonored, or insulted the poor man for whom Christ died. We see such an attitude towards the poor in today's society, but never should God's people who claim to be Christ-like manifest such a spirit of contempt for the poor of this world. On the other hand, God's Word does not teach one to dishonor the rich of this world either. 1 Peter 2:17 says, "Honour all men." Every person who comes into the assembly should be treated with respect, friendliness, and a warm welcome. The Gospel is God's power to save every individual, regardless of one's status in life.

Perhaps it should be noted at this point that the apostles and brethren did not fully understand that salvation was for all men. After the conversion of Cornelius, they realized salvation was for the Jew and the Gentile (Acts 10:34-48; Rom. 1:16). Today, we must preach the saving power of the gospel of Jesus Christ to everyone, the Jew and the Gentile, the rich and the poor, the educated and the uneducated, because all need the cleansing blood of the Lamb.

Do Not Rich Men Oppress You, And Draw You Before The Judgment Seats

Since they have dishonored the poor, James asks this question pointing to the gross wrong they had done by favoring the rich and insulting the poor. He seemingly uses this question to remind his fellow believers in Christ what customarily happens in the society of his day. The rich had violently dragged the poor into courts of law or before judgment seats and had them cast into prison, forcing them to pay their debt in full. Possibly James refers to the fact that the rich had oppressed them by dragging them before heathen tribunals sometimes because of their faith in the Son of God. James reminds his brethren that they were dishonoring the poor when they came into the assemblies just as the rich had dishonored them.

2:7—Do Not They Blaspheme That Worthy Name By The Which Ye Are Called

James provokes their thoughts by asking this question. The verse is saying these rich men are the ones who slander, speak evil of, or rail upon the worthy, honorable, and noble name of Jesus Christ. The answer would be an obvious "yes" to these three rhetorical questions, which the writer asks in verses 5-7. These were statements of truth concerning the persecutions of the early church.

The rich blaspheme the name of Christ today as it was in James' day. Perhaps these believers who were scattered abroad could remember their former treatment (Acts 8:3-4; 9:1-2). In Acts 26, Paul speaks before Agrippa about his former belief in the Jewish religion before his conversion and how he had thought he should do things contrary to the name of Jesus of Nazareth. He spoke of how he had punished the saints in Jerusalem by shutting them up in prison and had compelled them to blaspheme (Acts 26:11).

James is possibly reminding the brethren how they had insulted or dishonored the poor and honored the rich. It is so inconsistent for them to behave in such a manner. He reminds the brethren of "the worthy name" of Jesus Christ by which they were called. They had obeyed the gospel of Jesus Christ (Matt. 28:19; Acts 2:38) in their conversion to that worthy, holy, honorable name of Jesus Christ. Men and women are called by the same name of Jesus today (Rom. 1:16; Gal. 3:26, 27; Col. 2:10-13). They had been marked by the name of Christ and thus belonged to Christ and God (1 Cor. 3:23). Remember, in James 1:1, he also refers to himself as a servant of God and the Lord Jesus Christ. What a holy and honorable name Christians wear today!

Lesson Four Review Questions For Discussion (1:26-27 & 2:1-7)

Verse 26

1. Why is a religious person whose tongue runs loose like an unbridled horse deceived? _____

_____

2. Define "vain" religion. _____

_____

Verse 27

3. If "pure and undefiled religion" is the subject or theme of the entire book of James, how can one put this theme into practice in their life? _____

_____

_____

4. Who are two of the classes of people mentioned that cannot help themselves?

_____

5. How can one explain that there is more to being a Christian than just faithfully attending worship services of the church? _____

_____

_____

James ——

Verse 1

6. How does God view one's faith in Jesus Christ if one exhibits respect of persons?

_____

_____

Verse 2

7. Why is it unwise to make a judgment based on outward appearance? _____

_____

_____

Verse 3

8. What should be the proper procedure to welcome all visitors? _____

_____

_____

Verse 4

9. What does Jesus mean by "righteous" judgment (John 7:24)? _____

_____

_____

Verse 5

10. In what way has God "chosen the poor of this world rich in faith, and heirs of the kingdom?" _____

_____

Verse 6

11. How had they despised the poor? _____

_____

12. Why should the local church, above all other places, have equality among believers (John 13:34-35)? _____

_____

_____

Verse 7.

13. What does the phrase "the worthy name" by which all men are called mean?

_____

_____

14. What hymn comes to your mind when you understand just how worthy our Lord is to receive praises? _____

Lesson 5—James 2:8-13

~~~~~~~~~~~~~~~~~~~~~~~ Commentary and Questions

2:8—If Ye Fulfil The Royal Law According To The Scripture, Thou Shalt Love Thy Neighbour As Thyself

James calls the law of love "the royal law" because God commanded it in both the O.T. and N.T. It is unchangeable and timeless. Both God the Father and Jesus Christ, the Son of God, command this universal law, "thou shalt love thy neighbour as thyself." James reminds his fellow believers to "fulfil the royal law" or the kingly law meaning the supreme law of our God, which can also be read in Leviticus 19:18 and was repeated by our Lord in the gospels.

Jesus said, "Thou shalt love the Lord thy God with all thy heart, and with all thy soul, and with all thy mind. This is the first and great commandment. And the second is like unto it, Thou shalt love thy neighbor as thyself. On these two commands hang all the law and the prophets" (Matt. 22:37-40). Mark quotes our Lord, "There is none other commandment greater than these" (Mark 12:31b). These words can also be read today in Matthew 5:43; 19:16-19; Romans 13:9; Galatians 5:14, as well as James 2:8. Prejudice, partiality, and favoritism violate the Scriptures in both the old covenant and the new. If one loves their neighbor as oneself, one will not violate the Lord's teaching by dishonoring the poor, as stated in the previous verses.

Ye Do Well

If obedient believers keep the "royal law" found in the Scriptures, "Love thy neighbor as thyself," they are doing right. They do well if they adhere to this kingly law by fulfilling the Lord's command in all of their relationships with others. If believers treat their neighbors as they want to be treated, they will fulfill God's supreme law of love. How would they feel if upon entering a worship assembly someone told them to sit on the floor or stand by the wall, then gave a good seat to someone who appeared to be wealthy or prominent? It is certainly not fulfilling the royal law by showing contempt to others, especially if they appear to be poor or destitute. Would they be willing to give up their seat and sit on the floor or stand by the wall manifesting their love for their neighbor? Love is a keyword in this passage because charity or love never fails (1 Cor. 13:4-8).

2:9 But If Ye Have Respect To Persons, Ye Commit Sin, And Are Convinced Of The Law As Transgressors

James speaks plainly to those who show partiality, disrespect, or dishonor to the poor. By doing so, they are violating the royal law and sinning. John defines sin as a "transgression of the law" (1 John 3:4). The word convinced means one is convicted by law to be guilty of violating that law if one has respect of persons. James does not beat around the bush as the old saying goes but says straight forward, "if ye have respect to persons, ye commit sin."

In the case of Cornelius' conversion, after seeing the vision, the Apostle Peter realizes a truth concerning the conversion of the Gentiles (Acts 10). Peter then says a truth concerning God's character: "Of a truth, I perceive that God is no respecter of persons" (Acts 10:34). Peter is speaking of the Jews and Gentiles, whereas James is speaking of the rich and the poor. Showing favoritism towards the rich while disregarding the poor is a transgression of the law of liberty and the law of love. Christian people today cannot be respecters of persons and still be like our heavenly Father and our Lord Jesus Christ.

2:10—For Whosoever Shall Keep The Whole Law, And Yet Offend In One Point, He Is Guilty Of All

James issues a statement to illustrate the seriousness of the sin of showing partiality or oppressing the poor that no doubt gets the attention of the brethren. When one dishonors the poor, he is guilty of violating the royal law as a whole and becomes a lawbreaker. James is not saying a person violates every aspect of the law but rather violates the royal law itself. There are several illustrations that we could consider showing how one can violate the whole law by breaking it in just one point.

If a person today appeared in court for speeding, doing 75 mph in a 55 mph speed zone, he could not justify himself by saying to the judge, "Your honor, never do I fail to stop at a stop sign, run a red light, drive while under the influence of alcoholic beverages or illegal drugs, text while driving, or exhibit road rage." The judge would likely say, "Yes, I understand that you never practice all those acts of unsafe driving, but you have become a lawbreaker by speeding, thus violating the law."

Other examples: If any part of a person's body is leprous, the whole person is regarded as a leper. If a person commits fornication just one time, does he not become a fornicator? How many times does a person become intoxicated before he is guilty of the sin of drunkenness? Does he not become a violator of Galatians 5:19-21 and thus becomes a transgressor of the N.T. law of Christ? If one link out of a 20 foot chain is broken, is not the whole chain broken?

If Christians stumble in one point of God's law, it does not mean they are guilty of transgressing all the laws of God, but they do become lawbreakers by violating just one aspect of God's divine laws.

2:11—For He That Said, Do Not Commit Adultery, Said Also, Do Not Kill. Now If Thou Commit No Adultry, Yet If Thou Kill, Thou Art Become A Transgressor Of The Law

Any reasonable person, who lived under the Law of Moses, could not have misunderstood James' illustration. He uses two of the ten commandments to show how one can keep the other commandments yet violate the whole law by violating just one of these two laws. These two sins are also found in the N.T. law in many passages. Read Mark 10:11-12; Luke 16:18; Galatians 5:19-21. Either one of these sins, when committed, makes one a transgressor of the law of Christ. By context, James concludes that if believers dishonor or disrespect the poor by showing favoritism to the rich, they still have violated the royal law of loving their neighbor as themselves and thus become transgressors of the law of Christ.

2:12—So Speak Ye, And So Do, As They That Shall Be Judged By The Law Of Liberty

James exhorts all faithful believers to speak and act, in word or deed, by conforming to the law of liberty. In all manners of conduct, whatever one says or does, one must give an account. One must learn kindness of speech and kindness in one's actions by manifesting love toward one another because the "law of liberty" will be judge everyone.

James uses the word "law" numerous times in his letter to the faithful brethren. The word "law" refers to the Scriptures, which consist of separate commandments. It is written in the Scriptures that we must all stand or appear before the judgment seat of Christ (Rom. 14:10; 2 Cor. 5:10). God created man as a free moral agent; thus, he has the freedom to keep the law or violate it, but judgment will be based upon what the N.T. law requires of each person (Rev. 20:12-15).

In the preceding verses and this passage, we read the words law (2:8-12), the law of liberty (2:12), the perfect law of liberty (1:25), and the royal law (2:8). W.E. Vine's Dictionary of N.T. Words defines "law" (Gr. nomos) as that which means the rule or standard; "law of liberty" means freedom. When one obeys the gospel of Christ, the blood of Christ cleanses them. His blood washes away sin and sets the guilty free from sins committed against God. The word "perfect" (Gr. teleion) means full or completeness. The word royal (Gr. basilikos) means belonging to a king. All of these laws are referring to the N.T. law of Christ or the laws of the new covenant.

Other inspired writers speak of the O.T. law as a law of bondage. We are reminded that being under the N.T. law of Christ not only frees us from the bondage of sin but also from "the handwriting of ordinances that was against us, which was contrary to us, and took it out of the way, nailing it to his cross" (Col. 2:14). Obedient believers in Christ, no longer should allow anyone to bind these O.T. ordinances such as eating of meats, observing holy days, and keeping the Sabbath days. These ordinances were a foreshadow of the new covenant. The N.T. law of Christ will judge everyone who has lived on this side of the cross, thus being "judged by the law of liberty" that James speaks of in this verse. Paul wrote to the Galatians, "Stand fast therefore in the liberty wherewith Christ hath made us free, and be not entangled again with the yoke of bondage" (Gal. 5:1).

2:13—For He Shall Have Judgement Without Mercy, That Hath Shewed No Mercy

The word "mercy" (Gr. *eleos*) "is the outward manifestation of pity; it assumes need on the part of him who receives it, and resources adequate to meet the need on the part of him who shows it" (W.E. Vine's Dictionary). Any Christian today, as well as believers in James' day, who fails to show pity, will not receive mercy in the judgment. Showing pity is a Biblical principle found throughout the O.T and N.T. Scriptures and is taught by our Lord and Master. Read these comparable verses: Proverbs 3:3; 21:13; 2 Sam. 22:26-27; Micah 6:8; Matt. 6:14-15; 18:23-35; Luke 6:36.

Possibly James had the same principle in mind as Jesus did when He taught His disciples saying, "Blessed are the merciful: for they shall obtain mercy" (Matt. 5:7). James seems to have in mind the treatment of the poor who had been dishonored in previous verses. The warning here is a sobering truth by our Lord and also repeated by James. When those who profess to be obedient disciples stand before the judgment seat of Christ, not having shown mercy towards others, mercy will not be extended to them. One certainly cannot walk through the gates into the beautiful city of heaven without the mercy of the Lord. How sad it will be for those in the judgment who failed to extend mercy to others! How can one plead for the mercy of the Lord when one has shown no mercy to others?

And Mercy Rejoiceth Against Judgement

James means mercy triumphs over judgment. He seems to illustrate what our Lord said in Matthew 5:7. Mercy will prevail over judgment when obedient believers stand before the judgment of God, and the Lord will extend mercy to them only if they have manifested pity and have shown compassion on others. The question everyone should ask is this: When I stand in judgment, will I be pleading for strict justice for myself, or will I be pleading for mercy? Judgment will render justice and condemnation to the unmerciful. God will not overlook the smallest deed of showing mercy. The follower of Christ that gives "a cup of cold water only in the name of a disciple, verily I say unto you, he shall in no wise lose his reward" (Matt. 10:42).

Read the explanation of Paul as he wrote concerning a man named Onesiphorus in 2 Timothy 1:16-18. He and his house had shown mercy to Paul by diligently seeking him out while he was in Rome and in chains, often refreshing him. Paul recorded in 2 Timothy 1:18, "The Lord grant unto him that he may find mercy of the Lord in that day: and in how many things he ministered unto me at Ephesus." Paul also confirms mercy on that day, the same as James does (2:13).

God is rich in mercy (Eph. 2:4), and we can see how it prevails over justice in the saving of sinful man. One can easily see His love, grace, and mercy in His plan of salvation. Justice demands the condemnation of the sinner, but mercy pleads that one may be saved, and thus mercy prevails. One can understand God's love, grace, and mercy when one by faith obeys (Acts 2:38, Rom. 6:3-7, and Col. 2:11-13). Both God's justice and His mercy are satisfied when one by faith obeys the gospel of Jesus Christ.

Lesson Five Review Quesitons For Discussion (2:8-13)

Verse 8

1. What is the "royal law" and what are some ways of fulfilling it? _____

_____

_____

Verse 9

2. In what ways can one can sin by showing respect of persons? _____

_____

_____

Verse 10

3. How can one keep the law in many ways, transgress in one point, and become a transgressor or a lawbreaker of all the law? _____

_____

_____

Verse 11

4. How were the brethren to whom James is writing familiar with these two particular sins in his illustration? _____

_____

5. Why does one become a transgressor of the N.T. law if one commits either of these sins today? _____

_____

Verse 12

6. How did those to whom James wrote violate the "law of liberty" or the "law of love"? _____

_____

Verse 13

7. What is the meaning of "mercy" and how does it triumph over judgement? ____

_____

_____

8. What will judgment be like for one who is not willing to forgive others of their trespasses (Matt. 6:14-15)? _____

_____

_____

Lesson 6—James 2:14-26

~~~~~~~~~~~~~~~~~~~~~~~~~~ Commentary and Questions

2:14—What Doth It Profit, My Brethren, Though A Man Say He Hath Faith, And Have Not Works? Can Faith Save Him

James asks his Jewish brethren, members of the early N.T. church, two rhetorical questions in this passage concerning their faith and works. The answer to both is no. James condemns faith only, or a belief of mental assent, which will not save unless one's faith in Jesus Christ (2:1) and manifests good works in obedience to God's righteousness. Genuine faith will always manifest itself in acts of obedience. Lip service is of no value without obedience.

He addresses "brethren" who had already obeyed the Gospel of Jesus Christ, as is recorded in Acts 2. He identifies them as "my brethren" (Jews and proselytism - Acts 2:10). While in Jerusalem, most of them had heard the Gospel, had believed, and were obedient to the Apostle's doctrine (Acts 2:38, 47). Because of persecution, they were now scattered abroad outside Palestine (Acts 8:1). James reproves those who were converts of Christ and were claiming to have faith but were lacking in good works.

James refers to the works that God appointed unto man to do to be pleasing and acceptable in His sight. Genuine faith must also be accompanied by doing, as seen in 1:22 and 1:27. Although they were claiming to have faith, it is apparent that some were lax in such things as visiting the fatherless and widows in their afflictions, failing to manifest good works according to God's righteousness, showing partiality to the rich while dishonoring the poor, and failing to keep themselves unspotted from the world. In verse 12, James says, "so speak, and so do, as they that shall be judged by the law of liberty."

They were to obey every commandment of God (1:21-27; 2:1-13). He insists that one must be a doer of the word and that an active faith must manifest good works is the kind of faith that is pleasing to God. Faith and works must be maintained and are vital to the salvation of any professed believer as James illustrates in the next several verses of this epistle. Likewise, today, any Christian who fails to maintain a working faith cannot expect continual cleansing from sin, as found in 1 John 1:7. Paul states, "For we are his workmanship, created in Christ Jesus unto good works, which God hath before ordained that we should walk in them" (Eph. 2:10). Read John 15:8 and Titus 2:14. How futile it is for Christians to say they have faith, and at the same time, fail to maintain a pattern of scriptural works!

Some false religious theories of today would have you believe there is a contradiction in James' writings and the Apostle Paul's writings, which is not true. James is not contradicting Paul's writings concerning salvation by faith and good works. Both writers use Abraham as an example of a person who hears God's commands and then obeys. Paul addresses the person's justification in God's sight before and after his conversion, while James is addressing the faith of the believer after conversion. From this standpoint, James is saying faith without works is dead being alone (2:23). James and Paul approached faith and works from different points of view.

There are different kinds of works mentioned in the Bible: (1) Satan's works (1 John 3:8), (2) Man's works (Rom. 3:19, 20; Eph. 2:8,9), (3) God's works (John 6:28, 29). James deals with faith and works of the obedient believer while Paul addresses those who attempt to justify themselves by some other means rather than through faith in Jesus Christ and His shed blood. In his epistle to the Romans, Paul was discussing certain works of the Law of Moses that cannot justify, read Romans 3:28; 4:1-5; and Acts 13:38-39. He was addressing those of his day who were denying that active faith in Jesus Christ will save one from sin while some were also binding specific works of the O.T. law to be justified. In Ephesians 2:8, he is addressing the works of human merit that could not deserve the gift of Christ. For those who will be judged by the N.T. Law of Christ, faith is the instrument of salvation, but genuine faith that saves is a faith that obeys God's commandments (Heb. 5:8-9). There are no contradictions among any of the N.T. writers (2 Tim. 3:16, 17).

It is so sad that millions of people today are being misled by a man-made theory of a plan of salvation, which they call the "sinner's prayer." Certain denominational clergymen cherry-pick certain Scriptures written by Paul while taking them out of context, attempting to devise a plan of salvation by "faith only." By doing so, they contradict other plain passages of Scripture, which are essential to man's salvation, such as Acts 22:16; Romans 6:3-4; Galatians 3:26-27; Colossians 2:11-13. Paul gives a solemn warning to those who obey another gospel rather than the true Gospel of Jesus Christ (2 Cor. 4:3-4; 11: 4; Gal. 1:6-8).

2:15-17—If A Brother Or Sister Be Naked, And Destitue Of Daily Food. (V.16) And One Of You Say Unto Them, Depart In Peace, Be Ye Warmed And Filled, Notwithstanding Ye Give Them Not Those Things Which Are Needful To The Body; What Doth It Profit? (V. 17) Even So Faith, If It Hath Not Works, Is Dead, Being Alone

James, for his illustration of faith and works, selects members of the household of faith. He chooses an illustration that is strong and one that believers can easily understand. When a member sees a "brother or sister" of the church in need of clothing and daily food, says I will pray to God for your needs, but does not help those who are in need, James asks, "What doth it profit?" In other words, what benefit are you to them concerning the needful things of the body?

James likens one who turns away without fulfilling their needs unto one who has a dead faith. The text says plainly, "Even so faith, if it hath not works, is dead, being alone." James reminds us of our Lord's teaching about the person who stands before Christ in judgment and will be condemned (Matt. 25:31-46). Also, John writes, "But whoso hath this world's good, and seeth his brother have need, and shutteth up his bowels of compassion from him, how dwelleth the love of God in him? My little children, let us not love in word, neither in tongue; but in deed and in truth," (1 John 3:17-18). Genuine faith, when accompanied with good deeds, is not faith alone. Therefore, genuine faith is alive and not dead. It is the same today for Christians; no one should expect to walk through the gates into the beautiful city of Heaven who has a dead faith.

2:18—Yea, A Man May Say, Thou Hast Faith, And I Have Works: Shew Me Thy Faith Without Thy Works, And I Will Shew Thee My Faith By My Works

James uses another illustration to further enforce what he said in the previous verses (15-17). One man may claim loyalty to God by faith alone, while another supports his claim by promptly obeying God's instructions. Another can say, "I show my faith by my works; this is my way of proving I have faith. How are you going to prove your faith if you don't have works? What other proof can there be of one's faith if there are no fruits of faith? I can show you by my works a justifying, saving faith by being a 'doer of the word' (1:22)." One who claims to have faith can have a profession of faith in word only. One who has genuine faith will always manifest obedience to the will of God. No doubt, God sees faith in action when He sees one's good works that glorify Him.

In James 1:22-24, James admonishes the Christians concerning some of the good works they should be faithfully practicing to be a doer of the word and a doer of the work. One is to practice pure and undefiled religion in God's sight by visiting and assisting the fatherless and widows in their afflictions (1:27). James admonishes Christians to greet all visitors in the assembly without showing partiality (2:1-7). Faithful believers are to fulfill the royal law by loving their neighbors as themselves (2:8). A faithful believer is to assist a brother or sister in the church who needs daily necessities (2:15). A faithful Christian will always maintain a watchful eye while tending to the needs of others (2:16-18). Read Paul's admonishment in Galatians 6:10 concerning doing good unto all men, especially those of the household of faith. Read also the list of good works that Christian women are to teach younger women in the realm of the home (1 Tim. 5:10). Read Paul's and Peter's instructions concerning steadfastness (1 Cor. 15:58; Gal. 5:1; Phil. 1:27; 1 Pet. 5:9; 2 Pet. 3:17).

2:19—Thou Believest That There Is One God; Thou Doest Well: The Devils Also Believe, And Tremble

"Thou believest that there is one God" was the fundamental belief of those who practiced Judaism as well as those who professed to be followers of Jesus Christ (see Deut. 6:4; Mark 12:29). James likens the person who claims to have faith without manifesting works to the demons who also believe in the existence of the one true God of heaven. The demons believe there is one God and tremble or shudder. James uses the demons as proof that believing in God or simply mental assent is not saving faith. That is why the demons are not saved.

Jesus also states the importance of belief in God when he declared, "Ye believe in God, believe also in me" (John 14:1). Demons recognize the existence of the one true God and tremble at the realization that He will eventually consign them to everlasting fire prepared for the devil and his angels (Matt. 25:41-46). Read the words of the demons concerning their belief in the one God and His Son Jesus Christ, Who will be the judge of their eternal destiny (Matt. 8:29; Mark 1:24; Acts 19:15). "It is a fearful thing to fall into the hands of a living God" (Heb. 10:31). One must demonstrate one's faith with obedient works of God's righteousness.

Some Bible students understand this statement of James concerning the belief of the demons may imply a touch of irony in his words "thou believe that there is one God; thou doest well," as meaning so what, so do the demons! What superiority do you have over them because you confess your belief in the one true God and yet fail to put your faith into action? James aptly describes such an inactive, dead faith as the same kind of faith manifested by the demons. Jesus' words in Luke 6:46 are appropriate here: "And why call ye me Lord, Lord, and do not the things which I say?" Mark 7: 6 records Jesus' words, "Well hath Esaias prophesied of you hypocrites, as it is written, This people honoureth me with their lips, but their heart is far from me." James stated that some have the same kind of belief that demons have; they recognize the identity of the Lord but fail to do the things He says.

2:20—But Wilt Thou Know, O Vain Man, That Faith Without Works Is Dead

The ASV reads, "But will thou know, O vain man, that faith apart from works is barren?" The word vain is from the Greek word *kenos* literally meaning empty (W.E. Vines Dictionary). James continues his teaching concerning faith and works. He says to the vain man who boasts of his faith while lacking in good works, that kind of faith is barren, empty, useless, and unprofitable. James considers one that claims to have faith but no works to be vain and without biblical understanding. Likewise, a Christian today whose spiritual life is void of good works of obedience, cannot expect to hear our Lord say in the judgment, "Well done, thou good and faithful servant" (Matt. 25:21).

2:21—Was Not Abraham Our Father Justified By Works, When He Had Offered Isaac His Son Upon The Altar

Moses records the account of Abraham being justified by works in Genesis 22: 1-12. God commanded Abraham to offer his son Isaac upon the altar as a sacrifice. He did not hesitate to obey God's command. One can only imagine what went through Abraham's mind when he was given this command by God to offer his son, the seed promise of which God would raise a great nation. He did not question how God would keep His promise if his son were dead. Abraham went to the place where God told him and built an altar there. He bound his son Isaac, laid him upon the altar of wood, and stretched forth his hand with the knife to slay his son. The angel of the Lord called unto him out of heaven and said, "lay not thine hand upon the lad, and neither do thou anything unto him: for now I know that thou fearest God, seeing that thou hast not withheld thy son, thy only son from me" (Gen. 22:2). Although the angel stayed his hand from literally slaying Isaac, in the purpose of mind, Abraham offered up his son (Heb. 11:17-19).

2:22—Seeth Thou How Faith Wrought With His Works, And By Works Was Faith Made Perfect

James uses Abraham's faithfulness to illustrate being a doer of God's word and to show how, by his works, his faith was made perfect or brought to completion. He was willing to do anything and everything that God required of him. Read Genesis 22:15-18. The obedience of Abraham was an act of faith that he exercised in offering up his son. Neither faith alone nor works alone can make one justified, but God is pleased when faith and works of obedience operate in relationship one with the other.

It is no different for Christians today, for Jesus also taught the same obedience: "If any man will come after me, let him deny himself, and take up his cross, and follow me. For whosoever will save his life shall lose it: and whosoever will lose his life for my sake shall find it (Matt. 16:24-25). Disciples today must love the Lord by putting Him first and foremost and by faithful obedience to Him even before their own families (Luke 14:26, 33). Obeying the command of God brought Abraham's faith to completion, "made perfect." Read Genesis 22:1-19 and Hebrews 11:17-19.

2:23—And The Scripture Was Fullfilled Which Saith, Abraham Believed God, And It Was Imputed Unto Him For Righteousness: And He Was Called The Friend Of God

Abraham leaves us a legacy of one who was both a hearer and a doer! He heard God's every command then obeyed. When God called his name, Abraham replied, "Here I am Lord," then he obeyed God's instruction without hesitation. He was always willing to obey the most difficult commands. At God's instruction, he was willing to sacrifice his only son of promise, thus manifesting an obedient faith by his works. It was after Abraham offered his son Isaac upon the altar that "the Scripture was fulfilled" which said, "Abraham believed God," and his belief was "imputed unto him for righteousness." Imputed means reckoned or put to one's account. Abraham was indeed "the friend of God" (read 2 Chron. 20:7; Isa. 41:8). The Greek word for friend is *philos*, primarily an adjective, denoting loved, dear, or friendly, which came to be used as a noun in this passage and other N.T. passages (see W.E. Vine's Dictionary). Likewise, Jesus said to His disciples, "Ye are my friends, if ye do whatsoever I command you" (John 15:14). If everyone who professes Christianity would manifest this type of obedient faith, then all could be called "the friend of God."

2:24—Ye See Then How That By Works A Man Is Justified, And Not By Faith Only

In light of Abraham's justification by faith at work in the offering up of Isaac, "and not by faith only," James reminds his brethren of the obvious conclusion that they too are justified by a faith wrought in works, a faith that obeys God's will, and not by faith alone. Anyone who has mental or intellectual assent but does not bring one's faith to maturity by obedience has an inactive or dead faith. James affirms that no matter what pretended faith a man has, if it is not a faith that is adapted to produce good works of obedience, it is of no value in the matter of continual justification of the believer.

A Christian today is shown to be a true believer in Jesus Christ when he/she manifests obedience "and not by faith only" or mere profession or intellectual assent (Luke 6:46). Read what Jesus says about those who only profess Him by mental assent or lip service at the judgment (Matt. 7:21). The wise man is one that not only hears the sayings of Jesus but does them (Matt. 7:24-27). James refers to the works that God appointed man to do to be pleasing and acceptable in His sight. Doing God's works is called an obedient faith. Read what the Hebrew writer said concerning obedience to Christ (Heb. 5:8-9).

2:25—Likewise Also Was Not Rahab The Harlot Justified By Works, When She Had Received The Messengers, And Had Sent Them Out Another Way

The second illustration is "Rahab the harlot," who exemplified faith by receiving God's messengers and sending them out another way. James uses an example of a harlot who had obeyed God, turned her life around, and manifested her faith by good works: namely protecting God's messengers. She showed by her actions that her faith was genuine and not just mental assent. Her actions showed that she truly believed God and by her works was justified, accounted righteous by God(Joshua 2:1-21, 6:17, 22-25).

We don't know why James chose this Canaanite harlot's faith other than by inspiration. He uses her example to show how a sinful person can change from disobedient faith to an obedient faith that exemplified her active faith by her works. Regardless of the sinful life people live, when they obey God, their lives can bring forth works that demonstrate an active faith. This kind of faith produces godliness and contentment that glorifies God (Rom. 8:33-34; 1 Cor. 1:30-31). "By faith, the harlot Rahab perished not with them that believed not, when she had received the spies with peace" (Heb. 11:31). It is nonetheless true today that the obedient active faith of a Christian will manifest works of kindness and mercy, and he/she will not perish with those whose faith is inactive and disobedient to our Lord's instructions (Matt. 25:31-46).

2:26—For As The Body Without The Spirit Is Dead, So Faith Without Works Is Dead Also

James uses an easily understood picture of a physical human body being dead, inactive, and lifeless when the body is separated from the spirit. When one's faith is separated from obedience, it is lifeless as a dead body from which the spirit has departed. The dead body is like a Christian today who claims to have faith, yet lacks works, being dead also. James seems to remind his readers of the statement made in 2:17. He reemphasizes the truth of v. 17 to that of a decaying corpse likened unto a believer whose faith is inactive. When our Lord is in the midst of His churches of Asia, and views each member of the church, what does He see (Rev. 2:19)? To all, He says, "I know thy works." Another illustration that we can all relate to is faith compared with a well-tuned engine in a car. The life of a beautiful vehicle is the engine; thus, a car without a motor is useless. "So faith without works is dead also."

Lesson Six Review Questions For Discussion (2:14-26)

Verse 14

1. Why can't an inactive faith save anyone? _____

_____

Verses 15-17

2. Describe some things an active faith does concerning the church where one is a member? _____

_____

3. What should one do if one sees another Christian in need of clothing , food, or other such daily necessities? _____

_____

4. What is a dead faith? _____

_____

Verse 18

5. What is the difference in the faith of one who just claims to have faith and one
   shows their faith by works? _____

_____

Verse 19

6. What do the demons illustrate about faith and works? _____

_____

Verse 20

7. Who does James say is a vain man? _____

8. How can one improve their faith in God's sight? _____

_____

Verses 21

9. Describe Abraham's faith. _____

_____

Verse 22

10. How was Abraham's faith made perfect or brought to completion? _____

_____

_____

Verse 23

11. Why did God call Abraham His friend? _____

_____

Verse 24

12. How can Christians today let their faith die? _____

_____

Verse 25.

13. What can a sinner learn from Rahab's faith? _____

_____

_____

Verse 26.

14. What are some examples today of faith that is like a body separated from the spirit? _____

_____

_____

Chapter 3

~~~~~~~~~~~~~~~~~~~Analysis and Brief Summary

Vss.1-2
Public teachers are subject to greater condemnation.

Vss. 3-6
Three analogies likened to the size of the tongue compared to the whole body: The size of bits in a horse's mouth, the helm of a ship, and a small spark. Like the tongue, each is a small object that can cause great damage. The danger of sinning with this little member is pointed out and illustrated.

Vss. 7-8
James uses examples of beasts, birds, serpents, and sea animals that have been tamed by man, but the tongue cannot be tamed. The tongue is an unruly evil, full of deadly poison.

Vss. 9-12
Three analogies that are incompatible when compared to the uses and misuses of the tongue: blessing God and cursing our fellowman from the same source, a spring bringing forth fresh water and bitter, and the fig tree bearing the fruit of olives berries.

Vss. 13-16
The kind of wisdom that comes from above is the wisdom that teachers need: meekness of wisdom versus bitter envying and strife, heavenly wisdom versus earthly wisdom.

Vss. 17-18
The characteristics of godly wisdom that bring forth the fruit of righteousness.

Lesson 7—James 3:1-12

3:1—My Brethren, Be Not Many Masters, Knowing That We Shall Receive The Greater Condemnation

It is of great importance for the Bible student to notice that the inspired writer is about to introduce the subject of the misuses of the tongue (3:1-12). He previously alluded to this subject by instructing his fellow believers to be slow to speak in 1:19, 26, and also chapter 2 of this epistle emphasized the failure of talking without doing. James, in the next several verses, is about to focus on words rather than works. In this discourse on the tongue, he is addressing each member of the church, especially the teachers.

James addresses his brethren, fellow Jewish believers of the first century church. These "masters" mentioned here (KJV) are teachers. The ASV translates this verse, "Be not many of you teachers, my brethren, knowing that we shall receive heavier judgment." Teach (Gr. *didasko*) means to give instructions (W.E. Vine's Dictionary). One can find "teach" or "teachers" in numerous passages in the N.T. The Bible refers to Jesus and others as "teacher" (Acts 13:1; 1 Cor. 12:28, 29; Eph. 4:11). Hebrews 5:12 says, "For when for the time ye ought to be teachers," meaning all should eventually become teachers in some capacity.

James gives warning to those teachers in the first century as well as now because teachers will receive the "greater condemnation" or stricter judgment. One reason for harsh judgment is because they can lead the souls of the people astray by false teaching. Another reason they will be judged with strictness is because of their influence on others by the example they set. James is not saying this to discourage individuals from becoming teachers but gives warning to teachers that by their example and doctrine that they not only endanger the souls of others but also their own soul.

Local churches always need qualified teachers, then as well as today. The Scriptures contain more instructions for qualified teachers and evangelists than for the qualifications of the elders and deacons. After many hours of study and preparation, anyone who desires this honorable work of becoming a teacher should do so with zeal and a pure manner of life. A teacher of the gospel should examine his motives for desiring this work: it should be for the sake of saving his own soul as well as the souls of others who hear him (1 Tim 4:16). Becoming a teacher should be entered into with proper intentions and qualifications: knowledge, manner of life, ability, and zeal with a desire to proclaim the Gospel of Jesus Christ. A teacher's main objective is to win the lost and edify the saved by using sound doctrine in a pure manner (Eph. 4:29; Col. 4:6; 2 Tim. 2:2; Titus 2:8).

Paul spoke of men who would heap to themselves teachers who would tell people just what they wanted to hear (2 Tim. 4:3). Unqualified teachers cause great damage to Christ and His church then as well as today (Matt. 23:6-8; Acts 20:29-30; 2 Peter 2:1-3). Any teacher or preacher will receive the greater condemnation because he must not only practice what he preaches but will give an account for his manner of speech as well (Col. 4:6; 1 Peter 3:15-16). One who teaches or preaches a "perverted gospel" will receive condemnation (Gal. 1:6-9; Matt. 18:6-7).

3:2—For In Many Things We Offend All

Every person is guilty at one time or another of offending. All have been guilty of sin because all are guilty before God. When one realizes one has transgressed God's laws, one must be willing to pause immediately and pray for forgiveness, correct those offenses where possible, and put a bridle on the tongue. James uses the word "we" which would include him with all those to whom he is writing.

The ASV says, "in many things we all stumble." He elaborates upon one of the former themes of "swift to hear, slow to speak, slow to anger" (1:19). Every Christian today is to grow in this respect of becoming "slow to speak." James declares that a man who does not bridle his tongue has deceived himself in thinking he is religious in a manner that pleases God. Such a Christian has deceived his own heart, and thus his religion is vain (1:26). Any person who does not curb his tongue has a deeper problem within because Jesus taught that "out of the abundance of the heart the mouth speaketh" (Matt. 12:34).

James also uses the word "all," referring to every believer whether he/she be young or older, a teacher, or one being taught. "Slow to speak" is one of the traits of character that everyone who professes to be a child of God must possess to grow toward perfection. Misusing words that come from the lips or tongue (Matt.12:36-37) is a challenge for all to overcome daily.

If Any Man Offend Not In Word, The Same Is A Perfect Man, And Able Also To Bridle The Whole Body

If Christians today want to become perfect, complete in the sense of becoming full-grown, they must bring their bodies into subjection to the will of Christ. They must understand how they can offend others by the misuse of their words. The person who does not stumble in his speech is a person of great virtue, a "perfect man." Such a one at this point in life will be able to control the whole body, thus bringing it into subjection. Every child of God must put a leash on the tongue, thus giving due caution to "bridle the whole body." James is going to teach us in the next several verses that the tongue gets involved in every sin that the body commits.

3:3—Behold, We Put Bits In The Horses' Mouths, That They May Obey Us; And We Turn About Their Whole Body

James uses three analogies to which his readers can relate to illustrate how small things can regulate or control larger objects (vv. 3-5). The first illustration is putting "bits in the horses' mouths." A bit is a small thing when compared to the size of a big horse, yet by the use of a bit, one can "turn about their whole body" or bring about obedience and restraint. By the proper use of this small object, the rider can turn a big horse in the chosen direction. The horse then is controlled the same way people control their bodies by bridling their tongues. The person who has the proper restraint of his/her tongue can govern the whole body and thus bring it into subjection.

3:4—Behold Also The Ships, Which Though They Be So Great, And Are Driven Of Fierce Winds, Yet Are They Turned About With A Very Small Helm, Whithersoever The Governor Listeth

James now uses the analogy of a small rudder guiding a large ship. Even as fierce winds drive the great ship, the "governor" steers the great ship in the right direction. The ship is "turned about with a very small helm." A large seagoing vessel with its capacity to carry heavy loads of cargo can be swept away from the right course by fierce winds, but a small object like the helm can correct the course of the ship. Likewise, one should bring one's body into subjection by proper use of the tongue. These analogies of bits in a horse's mouth and a rudder of a ship illustrate the control of large things by the correct use of small objects by which the inspired writer relates to the proper use of the tongue.

3:5—Even So The Tongue Is A Little Member, And Boasteth Great Things. Behold, How Great A Matter A Little Fire Kindleth

Like the small bit and rudder in comparison to the size of a large horse and a seagoing vessel, "even so the tongue is a little member, and boasteth great things." James insists that the tongue can cause great damage when he said, "Behold, how great a matter a little fire kindleth!" How many can remember the history of the entire city of Chicago burning due to one small flame? A small fire has the potential to develop into the total devastation of a whole city, the loss of thousands and thousands of acres of forest lands, and the loss of lives of animals and people. Likewise, James compares the destruction of a fire and the nature of the tongue when unleashed, which can cause mass destruction and accomplish so much evil among friends, families, churches, and nations.

3:6—And The Tongue Is A Fire,
A World Of Iniquity: So Is The Tongue Among Our Members,
That It Defileth The Whole Body

"The tongue is a fire" that can consume or destroy people's lives when it is un-restrained. Fire is useful in its place when used rightfully. James is pointing out the evil in which the tongue can be involved. It is in a class of its own, "a world of iniquity" or lawlessness in itself. It is unlike any other member of the physical body. James likens the tongue to a roaring blaze of fire, which is the source of destruction.

The misuse of the tongue "defileth the whole body" as it can entice or influ-ence the whole body to sin. There is not one sin that the body commits in which the tongue doesn't incite or take part. Read Paul's list of "the sins of the flesh" (Gal. 5:19-21). The tongue can defile a person as our Lord warns: "that which cometh out of the mouth, this defileth a man" (Matt. 15:11). Remember, "If any man offend not in word, the same is a perfect man" (3:2). An unbridled tongue can result in the destruction of both body and soul in the torments of hell.

Some of the sins that our tongues can take part in are evil speaking, evil sur-mising, unwholesome criticism, speaking guile or bitterness, hatred, blas-phemy, deceit, boasting, bigotry, and covetousness. Peter gives Christians the recipe for having enjoyable days when he says, "For he that will love life, and see good days, let him refrain his tongue from evil, and his lips that they speak no guile" (1 Peter 3:10). The man whom God refers to as per-fect and upright before Him said, "My lips shall not speak wickedness, nor my tongue utter deceit (Job 27:4). The wise man said in the O.T., "Whoso keep-eth his mouth and his tongue keepeth his soul from troubles" (Proverbs 21:23).

The point to all that our Lord and the inspired writers of the N.T. Scrip-tures have to say on this matter is if one can curb their tongue, then one has dominion over the whole body. When the tongue speaks in favor of these sins, it can insight the whole body to sin. The tongue helps plan it, glory in it, defend it, and even comment on it after the sin is committed. Remember the wise man's counsel: "Suffer not thy mouth to cause thy flesh to sin" (Eccl. 5:6).

Consider gutter talk, filthy communication, vulgarity, or cursing. Remember our Lord's warning, "But I say unto you, That every idle word that men shall speak, they shall give account thereof in the day of judgment. For by thy words thou shalt be justified, and by thy words thou shalt be condemned" (Matt. 12:36-37). Wicked people spit-out these words as if there is no day of reckoning.

One of the most common sins among people today is gossip. The KJV uses the words, talebearer or whisperer, meaning the same thing. Gossip is a sin that ev-eryone has engaged in at one time or another. It is a favorite pastime for some; they love to hear the latest, which can be nothing but hot, juicy, sinful gossip.

Talebearing is defined as groundless rumors or idle talk about someone. A talebearer is one who bears these tales or groundless rumors that can alienate friendships, break up a family, or ruin a good person's reputation. This sin shatters the happiness of the innocent and "sows discord" among God's people, which He hates (Prov. 6:16, 19). A loose tongue can destroy the spirituality of others among the body of Christ also. In the Law of Moses, God forbids talebearing by saying, "thou shalt not go up and down as a talebearer among thy people" (Lev. 19:16). Also, "He that goeth about as a talebearer revealeth secrets: therefore meddle not with him that flattereth with his lips" (Proverbs 20:19). "A whisperer separateth chief friends" (Proverbs 16:28).

So, when someone comes with remarks such as "leave my name out of this," or "I don't know how true it is," or "I heard it through the grapevine," these remarks indicate what is being said is second hand and might not be the truth. Therefore we should immediately recognize it as gossip and reply, "Please don't cause me to sin by listening to unfounded rumors." The inspired wise man said, "A wicked doer giveth heed to false lips; and a liar giveth ear to a naughty tongue" (Proverbs 17: 4). Wicked people and liars love gossipers. If there are no itching ears, talebearing will soon cease.

Another common misuse of the tongue is euphemisms. Most Christians are aware of the sin of taking God's name in vain, but often use a shortened form of words without proper understanding. These are simply substitutes and are disrespectful toward God. Most are unaware of their everyday expressions, which could possibly result in sin if proper reverence is not spoken toward God. Some use these expressions daily in their vocabulary. When one sees something amazing or disgusting, they often use phrases such as "oh my God" or "omg," "lordy," "gosh," or "for Christ's sake." These are simply bywords or substitutes for using God's name in vain. One can find some of these expressions in Webster's Dictionary, where they are defined as euphemisms that refer to God's goodness. As harmless as they may appear, if used without proper reverence for deity, are they not in violation of Scripture? God gave this commandment to His people many centuries ago, "Thou shalt not take the name of the Lord thy God in vain: for the Lord will not hold him guiltless that taketh his name in vain" (Exodus 20:7).

And Setteth On Fire The Course Of Nature; And It Is Set On Fire Of Hell.

James states that the tongue is a fire, a world of iniquity or lawlessness. It is set among our members, staining the whole body, setting on fire the entire "course of nature." The ASV says, "wheel of nature." An individual who maintains a continual conversation of slander or misuse of their tongue will always be considered as being corrupt as if one has his tongue set on cruise control headed toward torment.

"Setteth on fire the course of nature" is explained by Barnes Notes as a "wheel of nature or anything made for revolving or running." Wheel of life starts at birth and runs on through one's entire period of life. It probably is referring to the individual's course of life that accomplishes the work of Satan by misuse of the tongue, which is "set on the fire of hell" (Gr. *Geenna* or Heb. *Ge-Hinnom*). Jesus said it was a place "prepared for the devil and his angels" (Matt. 25:41). In Revelation 21:8, John describes the wicked that "shall have their part in the lake which burneth with fire and brimstone: which is the second death." The conclusion to this passage in James 3:6 is that the unbridled tongue will only accomplish the work of Satan and will cause one to be eternally lost in hell.

3:7-8—For Every Kind Of Beasts, And Of Birds, And Of Serpents, And Of Things In The Sea, Is Tamed, And Hath Been Tamed Of Mankind: (V. 8) But The Tongue Can No Man Tame; It Is An Unruly Evil, Full Of Deadly Poison

We all stand amazed at how a man can take wild, vicious animals like the lion, tiger, or elephant and tame them. Humans can tame these wild animals to where they are no longer, for the most part, a threat to human beings. Man can even take certain species of birds and teach them to say certain words and train to hunt prey. Sea creatures like dolphins and other species are brought into captivity and can be taught to perform amazing feats. God gave man dominion over these animals (Gen. 1:26). "But the tongue can no man tame." A person can bridle, curb, or bring it into subjection, but once unleashed, it can again kill, wound, and destroy like a wild animal.

A man may tame wild beasts, but his tongue he cannot tame. He must always keep it under control by the use of proper restraints just as he does the animals. The tongue is "an unruly evil" if it is not properly restrained at all times. It is "full of deadly poison" like the venomous poison of a snake that can harm the human body, and so can the tongue wound or destroy the happiness and spirituality of others. Just a few unkind words can cause so much damage to others by destroying friendships, families, churches, nations, and ultimately man's entire wellbeing.

3:9—Therewith Bless We God, Even The Father; And Therewith Curse We Men, Which Are Made After The Similitude Of God

The ASV says, "Therewith bless we the Lord and Father; and therewith curse we men, who are made after the likeness of God." The tongue has the power to pronounce blessing or cursing, life or death (Prov. 18:21). Man's tongue is capable of praising God one minute and then the next minute cursing his fellowman, who is made in "the similitude of God." One can sing about the amazing grace of God or pray to the Heavenly Father seeking favors or blessings and then later with the same muscle disrespect people who are made in God's likeness. Blessing and cursing with the tongue is inconsistent use of it.

James includes himself and all believers. Does this not violate the royal law of love in 2:8? John also addresses this inconsistency, "If a man say, I love God, and hateth his brother, he is a liar: for he that loveth not his brother whom he hath seen, how can he love God whom he hath not seen? And this commandment have we from him, That he who loveth God love his brother also" (1 John 4:20-21).

3:10-12—Out Of The Same Mouth Proceedeth Blessing And Cursing. My Brethren, These Things Ought Not So To Be. (Vs. 11) Doth A Fountain Send Forth At The Same Place Sweet Water And Bitter? (Vs. 12) Can The Fig Tree, My Brethren, Bear Olive Berries? Either A Vine, Figs? So Can No Fountain Both Yield Salt Water And Fresh

3:10—The inspired writer makes his point very clear about brethren who use the same tongue to bless God and then curse or dishonor his brethren, which a member of the church should never do. James asks questions and uses several examples to provoke his brethren then or a Christian today of how absurd it is to do so. "Blessing and cursing" may be common and universal among worldly people, but these things should not be so among brethren. Christian people should always strive to improve the use of their tongue so that they will be consistently blessing their fellowman and well as God. It is not the true nature of a believer to allow blessing and cursing to proceed from the same mouth. "These things ought not so to be."

3:11—James provokes their thoughts by using the analogy of a "fountain," sending forth fresh spring water and bitter or salt water at the same well. How absurd it is for a tongue to utter praises unto God and with the same tongue utter words of hatred for others! Inconsistent use of the tongue is certainly not approved by God. The inspired writer finds this to be so unnatural and important that he repeats it at the conclusion of his teaching on the tongue in the next verse.

3:12—Does the fig tree naturally bear olive berries? Can the fruit that grows on vines be found growing on trees? Is this not contrary to nature or what our Creator intended? James uses this analogy to show how unnatural it is for a tree to bear both figs and olives or a vine to produce fruit that comes from a fig tree. These two illustrations are as opposed to one another as a brother in Christ praising God and cursing his fellowman from the same mouth. These illustrations show believers how their speech is inconsistent with their professed religion of godliness when they allow their tongues to run loose. If Christians today possess the true nature that God intends, they must use their tongues in a manner that only produces good fruit rather than stumbling blocks. James uses several analogies (verses 2-12) in his writings to impress upon their minds how they can sin with their tongues. These analogies elaborate upon what our Lord had taught His disciples that one's words are revealing what is in the heart, and thus the true character will be revealed by what comes from one's lips.

Lesson Seven Review Questions For Discussion (3:1-12)

Verse 1

1. Why will teachers receive the greater condemnation? _____

_____

Verse 2

2. What does it means to "offend" in word? _____

_____

3. Why does James used the word "we?" _____

_____

_____

Verse 3

4. How is putting a bit in a horse's mouth like putting a leash on one's tongue? ___

_____

Verse 4

5. How is a rudder controlling a ship is similar to the tongue controlling the body?

_____

_____

Verse 5

6. How can the wrong words result in mass destruction the same way a spark results in massive destruction? _____

_____

_____

Verse 6

7. How can the tongue defile or pollute the whole body? _____

_____

8. "Whoso _____ his _____ and his _____ _____his _____ from troubles," Proverbs 21:23.

9. Explain how the tongue takes part in the sins of the flesh listed in Galatians 5:19-21? _____

_____

_____

Verses 7 & 8

10. How is taming the tongue like taming a wild beast? _____

_____

_____

Verse 9

11. Why is praising God with one's tongue unacceptable if one is cursing others at the same time? _____

_____

Verses 10-12

12. Identify the two illustrations James uses to discuss how absurd it is to allow both blessing and cursing to proceed from the same mouth. _____

_____

_____

13. What can be learned from these illustrations regarding inconsistently using the tongue to bless and curse? _____

_____

Lesson 8—James 3:13-4:3

⧗⧗⧗⧗⧗⧗⧗⧗⧗⧗⧗⧗⧗Commentary and Questions

3:13—Who Is A Wise Man And Endued With Knowledge Among You? Let Him Shew Out Of A Good Conversation His Works With Meekness Of Wisdom

In this verse, James couples the words "knowledge" and "wisdom." He transitions his teaching from sins of the tongue to knowledge or understanding of God's word and meekness or gentleness of wisdom. The ASV says, "Who is wise and understanding among you?" Wise and understanding possibly have reference to anyone who desires to be a teacher of others (3:1). All Christians are to become teachers in some capacity (Heb. 5:12). One who becomes "endued with knowledge" is one who has been properly instructed by studying and rightly dividing the word of truth and by putting into practice those things which one has learned.

James uses two words that need attention: "knowledge" and "wisdom." Knowledge is what one has learned or acquired by understanding what the will of God is. He has possessed the truth and understands it. Wisdom is the ability to make proper application of that spiritual knowledge. This verse suggests that each teacher is to do a self-examination and determine whether he/she is truly wise with understanding and a worthy model of emulation. Most likely, some were lacking these qualities as Christians in the Lord's church do today.

The second part of this verse instructs the wise man who is endued with knowledge to put it to use with "meekness of wisdom." A wise believer will exhibit his/her knowledge and wisdom with good "works." Words are never enough without the beauty of holiness. A wise teacher will demonstrate wisdom by his/her godly conduct and by a meek or humble attitude. James exhorts his "beloved brethren" to "receive with meekness the engrafted word" (1:21). Peter also enjoins "meekness" in setting forth the grounds of the Christian's hope (1 Pet. 3:15).

James asks the question in this verse, "Who is a wise man among you?" A wise man is one who is willing to conform his life to the will of God by loving his neighbor as himself, growing in grace and knowledge, having a faith which displays good works, exhibiting godly behavior, having gentleness of wisdom, and maintaining a calm controlled spirit. Any teacher who aspires to be a soul winner by practicing meekness or gentleness of wisdom will never manifest the attitude of "skinning" rather than "winning" the lost or erring. Read comparable verses in Galatians 6:1; Ephesians 4:15; 2 Timothy 2:24-26; Titus 3:1, 2.

3:14—But If Ye Have Bitter Envying And Strife In Your Hearts, Glory Not, And Lie Not Against The Truth

The person who exhibits "bitter envying and strife" coming from the heart, cannot claim to have wisdom from above. Envy (Gr. *zelos*) desires to deprive another of what he/she has. Strife means contention and is the expression of enmity or may be understood as disputes. Some Greek words like *logomachia* mean strife of words (See Vines Expository Dictionary). It is a "lie against the truth," meaning these are forbidden by the word of truth. The ASV uses the words "bitter jealously and faction" which means a selfish spirit that seeks its own will or advantage. See Roman 2:8-9; 2 Corinthians 12:20. Bitter jealousy and faction in a person's heart is not God's kind of true wisdom, but only promotes strife, contention, rivalry, and wrangling that make brethren competitors rather than workers together with Christ.

3:15—This Wisdom Descendeth Not From Above, But Is Earthly, Sensual, Devilish

"Earthy" wisdom means it exists on earth. "Sensual" refers to natural appetite or passion. "Devilish" means demonic or satanic. Earthly wisdom has the characteristics that James mentions in verses 14-16. The KJV describes these worldly characteristics as bitter envying, strife, confusion, every evil work, earthly, sensual, and devilish. Earthly wisdom or viewing from a worldly perspective does not come from God or heaven but comes from the world, and its source is the devil. Read these comparable verses: 1 Corinthians 1:20; Colossians. 3:1-2.

3:16—For Where Envying And Strife Is, There Is Confusion And Every Evil Work

The ASV renders this verse, "For where jealousy and faction are, there is confusion and every vile deed." Where envying and strife, bitter jealously, and factionalism exists in a church, there will be confusion and every evil work or vile deed. These are the characteristics of earthly wisdom that are not from above. When these exist in a local congregation, the result will be disorder, chaos, and ungodly behavior.

Because of this, clicks tend to form in a church; they manifest a party spirit and promote segregation from the rest of the body. Clicks promote division and sow discord, which God hates. The factional spirit of worldly people almost always results in "confusion." This type of confusion is opposed to peaceable wisdom that James mentions in the following verse. One can see a good example of confusion and worldly devilish wisdom in the political arena of our federal and state governments. One can see earthly, worldly wisdom in society in general, but one should never see this kind of worldly wisdom in the body of Christ.

3:17—But The Wisdom That Is From Above Is First Pure, Then Peaceable, Gentle, And Easy To Be Entreated, Full Of Mercy And Good Fruits, Without Partiality, And Without Hypocrisy

In the previous verses, James gives us the outcome of earthly wisdom but now provides the characteristics of heavenly wisdom. The source of this kind of wisdom is from God. Here he describes wisdom from God as "first pure." Pure means clean, holy, and uncontaminated. Peaceable describes one who seeks to get along with others to maintain harmonious relationships among men; the opposite is a troublemaker. Gentle expresses one who is fair, reasonable, and forbearing with those who disagree. Easy to be entreated means willing to submit to others, not self-willed, to be compliant. Full of mercy means the outward manifestation of pity, compassion towards those who are in need or in distress. Good fruits denote good works or deeds. The one without partiality does not make distinctions or show respect of persons and treats all men alike. Hypocrisy denotes pretense; a hypocrite says one thing and does another. When one who has wisdom from God speaks, one does so wholeheartedly without pretense. (See W.E. Vine's Dictionary).

3:18—And The Fruit Of Righteousness Is Sown In Peace Of Them That Make Peace

Peace among brethren is what helps produce holiness. The peacemakers are the ones who produce the fruit of God's righteousness among a congregation of God's people. Some have referred to peace as being the seed-ground of holiness, and the peacemaker that sows peace will win its harvest. The fruit of righteousness or the result of heavenly wisdom is peace. James' teaching in this passage is in total agreement with our Lord's Sermon on the Mount concerning the blessedness of the peacemaker (Matt. 5:9). In the previous verses, James contrasted the characteristics of earthly wisdom, which produces bitter envying and strife in one's heart with that of heavenly wisdom, which yields peace and harmony among brethren (vv. 14-18). Who are the peacemakers in the church today? They are the individuals who possess the attributes of the heavenly wisdom and who speak and act without self-interest or selfish ambitions. When one understands the characteristics of heavenly wisdom that James mentions in these verses, most likely, the Beatitudes that Jesus taught in Matthew 5 will come to mind.

Chapter 4

~~~~~~~~~~~~~~~~~~~~~Analysis and Brief Summary

Vss. 1-2
James explains the source of conflicts, wars, and dissensions. Division can be traced to the "lust" of men.

Verse 3
James deals with praying without proper motives

Verse 4
Discusses how the desire of this world is enmity with God.

Verse 5- 6
Deals with envy as the result of lust in one's heart and God resists all those who are proud and gives grace to all of them who manifest humbleness (verse 6).

Vss. 7-10
Teaches that friendship with God is the solution to these problems.

Vss. 11-12
Jame issues warnings against speaking evil or defaming our brethren by playing God and becoming a judge. There is only one lawgiver.

Vss. 13-17
Christians must depend upon God's will because man's life upon earth swiftly passes. Leaving God out of one's plans is evil; therefore, to him, that knows to do good and does it not, it is a sin.

Lesson 8 continued (James 4: 1-3)

4:1—From Whence Come Wars And Fightings Among You? Come They Not Hence, Even Of Your Lusts That War In Your Members

The KJV and the ASV use the words "wars" and "fightings" which seem to be referring to quarrels and conflicts among brethren of the early church. The word fightings is always rendered in the plural (Gr. *Mache*), which means strivings or strife in some translations (see W.E. Vine's Dictionary). James is now ready to point out the causes for so much strife and warring among God's people. Among the brotherhood of believers, there are many internal disorders or conflicts such as animosities, quarrels, contentions, factions, or bickering, which result in hostility, division, and dissension. James gives the answer while asking thought-provoking questions, "Come they not hence, even your lusts that war in your members?" Don't they spring from lusts or the uncontrolled passions of individuals? Is it not due to the carnal nature of some who fail to control these lusts that cause them to go on the warpath with others? "For where envying and strife is, there is confusion and every evil work" (3:16).

Before the establishment of the N.T. church in the first century, there was constant warring among various factions of the Jewish faith, such as the Pharisees, Sadducees, Essenes, Samaritans, and Zealots, but James is dealing with the infighting of Jewish brethren of the early church. Lust or evil, selfish desires will result in envying and strife, warring or fighting among people whether it be in a local church, in state government, or on a national level. James seems to contrast 3:18 with 4:1. While wisdom from above produces peace (3:18), worldly wisdom produces these conflicts.

It is of great importance to note that certain peaceful disagreements are necessary and commanded in the Scriptures. Passages like Jude 3 or 1 Timothy 6:12 instruct Christians to contend earnestly for the faith and fight the good fight of faith whereunto one has been called. Every Christian has this responsibility to contend earnestly for the faith and take a stand for the truth.

4:2—Ye Lust, And Have Not

"Lust" (Gr. *epithumia*) denotes strong desires of any kind (see W.E. Vine's Dictionary.) James uses this word, which means evil desires, cravings for power, prestige, or wealth, and results in evil activity. Paul also addresses this evil, "Let not sin therefore reign in your mortal body, that ye should obey it in the lust thereof" (Rom. 6:12). Paul and James, both in strong language, point out that "lust" will not produce the desired righteous blessings from God.

Ye Kill, And Desire To Have, And Cannot Obtain: Ye Fight And War

The ASV says, "ye kill and covet." The inspired writer uses words that can penetrate the hearts of his readers. This brutal, murderous spirit in one's heart can lead to every kind of vile deed or evil work. The word kill can refer to taking a person's life or metaphorically to the assassination of the character or reputation of another. James repeats the expressions, "ye lust," "ye kill," "and desire to have and cannot obtain," "ye fight and war and have not." Lust is the source of all contention, fighting, and strife among your members. These evils, when conceived in one's heart, will never furnish true happiness or contentment that fulfills God's righteousness. All these sinful desires stem from covetousness or lust in one's heart. "Covetousness is idolatry" (Col. 3:5).

Yet You Have Not, Because Ye Ask Not.

James makes it abundantly clear to his readers that failure to receive blessings from God is because of a failed prayer life. If one does not value a blessing from God enough to pray for it, then one does not deserve God's favor. Paul reminds Christians, "Be careful for nothing; but in every thing by prayer and supplication with thanksgiving let your requests be made known unto God" (Phil. 4:6). Paul means one is to pray more and worry less. Peter says that "the eyes of the Lord are over the righteous and his ears are open unto their prayers" (1 Pet. 3:12). Read the comparable verses in Psalm 10:4; Matthew 26:41; Luke 18:1; 1 Thessalonians 5:17.

4:3—Ye Ask, And Receive Not, Because Ye Ask Amiss, That Ye May Consume It Upon Your Lusts

Some "ask amiss" or pray with the wrong motive in mind, praying because of greed rather than need. Asking amiss is praying with the view of self- indulgence and for the fulfillment of one's carnal appetites. Some folks seem dissatisfied with descent and comfortable living, which is not improper to desire. Still, they are always looking for more luxurious things to the point of never becoming satisfied and contented. "But godliness with contentment is great gain" (1 Tim. 6:6). Have you ever wondered what fuels the gambler who plays the lottery? Paul gives a warning, "But they that will be rich fall into temptation and a snare, and into many foolish and hurtful lusts, which drown men in destruction and perdition" (1 Tim. 6:9). Read and understand Proverbs 28:8-9.

LESSON EIGHT REVIEW QUESTIONS FOR DISCUSSION (3:13-18; 4:1-3)

Verse 13.

1. How does a wise man become endued with knowledge? _____

_____

2. Define "good conversation." _____

_____

Verse 14.

3. Bitter envying and strife in a believer's heart can make one a competitor with other Christians rather than workers together with Christ (T or F).

Verse 15.

4. What are the characteristics of earthly wisdom? _____

_____

5. Who is the ultimate source of earthly wisdom? _____

Verse 16.

6. What does earthly wisdom produce? _____

_____

Verse 17.

7. List the characteristics of heavenly wisdom from God. _____

_____

_____

Verse 18.

8. How can one become a peacemaker in the church where you are a member? __

_____

_____

4:1

9. What feuls "wars and fightings" among the brethren? _____

_____

4:2

10. Define the word "lust." _____

_____

11. Lust is the source of contention, fighting and strife among brethren (T or F).

4:3

12. What does it mean to "ask amiss?" _____

_____

13. What does "godliness with contentment" mean (1 Tim. 6:6)? _____

_____

_____

James ————————————————————————————

Lesson 9—James 4:4-10

~~~~~~~~~~~~~~~~~~Commentary and Questions

4:4—Ye Adulterers And Adulteresses, Know Ye Not
That The Friendship Of The World Is Enmity With God

James says that men or women who are unfaithful to their covenant with God become His enemy. The old and new covenants refer to those who become unfaithful by breaking their marriage vows as "adulterers and adulteresses." James seems to have in mind adultery in a spiritual or ethical sense, thereby becoming God's enemies.

Those in the text were breaking the N.T. covenant by loving the world more than God, and by indulging in worldly, carnal lusts, they were engaging in spiritual adultery. "The friendship of the world is enmity with God." Spiritual adultery means loving the things of this world more than loving God and doing His will (1 John 2:15). Jesus refers to those in His day or time as "an evil and adulterous generation" (Matt. 12:39). The New Testament portrays Christians as the bride of Christ (2 Cor. 11:2; Eph. 5:23; Rev. 19:7). The Old Testament refers to God as the husband of His people Israel, who were unfaithful to the covenant He had made with them. They played the harlot committing whoredom in so much as they made images of men and set oil and incense before them. God refers to their lewd actions as fornication because they had played the "whore" with the Egyptians, Philistines, and Assyrians (Jeremiah 3; Ezek. 16; Hosea 2). God says concerning them, "But as a wife that committeth adultery, which taketh strangers instead of her husband!" (Ezek. 16:32).

Think of the inner pain and agony in the heart of one who has been betrayed by an unfaithful spouse and must reckon with the fact that one is faithful to an adulterous mate. Can you imagine what God feels in His heart when he sees a Christian engaging in spiritual adultery or has a world-loving heart?

Whosoever Therefore Will Be A Friend Of The World
Is The Enemy Of God.

In 3:13-4:12, James seems to contrast two groups of people: friends of the world and the friends of God. Those who embrace the friendship of the world manifest earthly wisdom. Those who are friends of God embrace heavenly wisdom. James describes wisdom from above as pure, peaceable, gentle, full of mercy, without partiality or hypocrisy (3:17-18). Those who manifest wisdom of this world are those whose lives abound in bitter envying, strife, contention, confusion, and every evil work (3:14-16). Lust in the heart is the source of all these evils that result in these problems.

"A friend of the world" is one who sets their heart on worldliness. James describes one who is fashioned or is motivated by worldly desires as a "friend of the world." This person neglects his/her duty to our Savior and becomes the Lord's enemy. Though one may profess to be a Christian, in reality, one becomes a friend of the world by yielding to worldliness. Jesus reminds His disciples, "If ye love me, keep my commandments" (John 14:15). One cannot serve two masters by loving the world and loving God at the same time (Matt. 6:24).

4:5—Do Ye Think That The Scripture Saith In Vain, The Spirit That Dwelleth In Us Lusteth To Envy

Bible scholars and translators have difficulty with this verse, and most agree that it is difficult to say with certainty what the true meaning is. Two of the main problems are the words "scripture" and "spirit." There are various ways this Scripture can be punctuated, leading to different translations of this verse. Is James referring to a particular verse of Scripture in the O.T.? If so, where is it found? He may be referring to all the Scriptures that pertain to what he said in verses 4 and 5. Various translations emphasize this verse differently. Is he talking about the Holy Spirit or the human spirit? James could be referring to all the Scriptures in general.

I will assume but cannot say with certainty that the writer has his sight set on "envy" the last word of this verse. He has previously discussed envying and strife in 3:16 and other passages that refer to envy in the inner man. This verse seems to refer to "our spirit or disposition as we are by nature, and it is equivalent to saying that we are naturally prone to envy" (Barnes Notes). I believe everyone can agree that the human spirit is wrong when it lusts to "envy." Envy is used in a bad sense, which means to desire worldliness, which carnal people possess. Truly, "whosoever therefore will be a friend of the world is the enemy of God" as stated in verse 4. The Bible student today can read all the Scriptures in the O.T. as well as the N.T. and conclude that God is a jealous God when one allows worldliness to take one's focus from Him.

4:6—But He Giveth More Grace. Wherefore He Saith, God Resisteth The Proud, But Giveth Grace Unto The Humble

In verses 6-10, James offers solutions for the strife existing among the brethren. The reference here is no doubt to God, Who gives more unmerited favor to some to restrain or overcome the evil passions that reign among worldly men. A servant of Jesus Christ should never be influenced by these unrestrained passions that lead to envy and strife among brethren. "Wherefore he saith, God resisteth the proud, but giveth grace to the humble," means God resists or opposes the proud but shows favor to the humble. This verse probably has reference to God's instruction throughout the

Bible. Also, James may have Solomon's counsel in mind where the wise man said, "Surely he scorneth the scorners: but he giveth grace unto the lowly" (Proverbs 3:34).

The Lord resists "the proud" or scorns those who reject His counsel but extends grace (unmerited favor) unto the humble because the true servant of Jesus Christ most always abounds in doing God's will by being subject to God and keeping His commandments. So, the key to receiving "more grace" is to remain meek or "humble" in spirit and always obedient. Some Bible students seem to think James is providing an antidote to spiritual unfaithfulness: by obtaining God's grace, one can overcome these sins. "Moreover the law entered, that the offence might abound. But where sin abounded, grace did much more abound: That as sin hath reigned unto death, even so might grace reign through righteousness unto eternal life by Jesus Christ our Lord" (Rom. 5:20-21). Read these comparable verses which speak of God's grace (Rom. 5:1-2; 2 Cor. 9:8; 2 Pet. 3:18).

4:7—Submit Yourselves Therefore To God. Resist The Devil, And He Will Flee From You

Verses 7-10 list commands that tell obedient believers some ways of how they must submit themselves to God. By submitting to God's will, they can eliminate becoming a friend of the world by following after worldliness and becoming an enemy of God. Every Christian today has the responsibility of submitting to God as our Lord did (Heb. 5:8). People should submit to God because He created all. His rule is good for them, all resistance to God is futile, submission to God is necessary for salvation, and submission is the only way to have peace with God.

"Resist the devil" by fighting against him because God has promised that Satan will run. Believers must fight the good fight of faith by total submission to what God commands by what is written in the Scriptures. Jesus, the perfect example of resisting the temptation of the devil (Matt. 4), would continually reply, "It is written." Jesus resisted Satan in every form of temptation. Likewise, Christians today must "abstain from all appearance of evil" (1 Thess. 5:22). When they refuse to be partakers of anything that appears to be evil, then they are resisting the devil, putting him to flight. Paul admonishes the Ephesians to "put on the whole armor of God" (Eph. 6:11). Likewise, Peter advised, "Be sober, be vigilant; because your adversary the devil, as a roaring lion, walketh about, seeking whom he may devour: Whom resist steadfast in the faith, knowing that the same afflictions are accomplished in your brethren that are in the world" (1 Pet. 5:8, 9). Resisting the devil was one of the characteristics of Job, who the Bible accounts as "perfect and upright, and one that feared God and eschewed evil" (Job 1:1).

4:8—Draw Nigh To God, And He Will Draw Nigh To You

James instructs his readers to "draw nigh to God." The Greek word for "draw" is *engizo*, which means to approach or draw near (W.E. Vine's Dictionary). When one draws nigh to God, He then will "draw nigh to you." Drawing nigh to God is both an invitation and a promise from God to the obedient believer. Jesus said to those who would be his disciples, "Come unto me, all ye that labour and are heavy laden, and I will give you rest" (Matt. 11:28).

One draws near to God when one submits to the will of God in humble submission and obedience. Read 1 Chronicles 28:9 and Hebrews 10:22. There are many ways both young and older Christians today can become closer to God and His Son Jesus Christ: become a prayer warrior, spend more personal time studying the Scriptures, attend every possible worship service, visit the sick or elderly, and be a doer of the work that God has prescribed. All of these can enrich one's spiritual life as one develops the proper attitude towards total dependence upon God.

Cleanse Your Hands, Ye Sinners;
And Purify Your Hearts, Ye Double Minded

Cleansing of one's hands means cleansing a person's actions (deeds). Perhaps James has in mind the washing of one's hands in the reconciling actions of the O.T. worshipers and priests at the temple (Exodus 30:19-21; Lev. 16:4). In the N.T., the cleansing of one's hands and purifying one's heart are symbols of moral purity. Notice James combines cleansing of one's hands and purifying the heart. "Ye sinners" are unfaithful brethren. Some had separated themselves from God because their hands engaged in sinful acts.

When one draws nigh to God, it becomes necessary to obey the instructions recorded in 4:8-10. It takes both clean hands and a pure heart to be pleasing to God. When one cleanses their heart of evil thoughts, then one's actions or deeds will be purified or cleansed as well. Then and only then will God rule upon the throne of one's heart. A "double-minded" person is one with two minds. One part wants to live for the Lord while at the same time, one's actions are displeasing to God. A double-minded person is trying to straddle both sides of the fence. God requires purity in both word and deed. One's worship and service must be whole-hearted. No other service is acceptable before the Lord.

4:9—Be Afflicted, And Mourn, And Weep: Let Your Laughter
Be Turned To Mourning, And Your Joy To Heaviness

James' instructions are in total agreement with our Lord's teaching in his sermon on the mount where Jesus said, "Blessed are they that mourn: for they shall be comforted" (Matt. 5:4). "Be afflicted, and mourn, and weep" is because of one's sins and transgressions against God, which should bring about remorsefulness. James is no doubt talking about the right attitude that can bring about genuine repentance that the Lord requires from his unfaithful followers who are living lives of double-mindedness in the previous verse.

James mentions these deep acts of penitence when godly sorrow works genuine repentance in humble submission to the will of God. "Be afflicted" denotes the downcast, miserable, depressed feeling of those who were willing to turn from the sinful double standard that some of them were living. "Mourn" means the deep sadness of heart (Eccl. 7:3) concerning their sins when godly sorrow works repentance (2 Cor. 7:10-11). Ofttimes those who feel deep sadness of heart will mourn at the thought of their sins or course of wickedness. "Let your laughter be turned to mourning." Laughter or mirth is related to the pleasures of sin. "Joy to heaviness" is the sin once considered pleasurable or enjoyable now becomes heaviness of heart. "Heaviness" (*katepheia*) probably denotes a downcast look, expressive of sorrow (W.E. Vines Dictionary of N.T. Words).

4:10—Humble Yourselves In The Sight Of The Lord, And He Shall Lift You Up

Humility is the key to obtaining a rightful relationship with God. The penitent publican in the Lord's parable who was praying in the temple humbled himself in God's presence and "would not lift up so much as his eyes unto heaven" but humbly pleaded for God's mercy (Luke 18:13). James taught those who were believers that needed to repent of doublemindedness (4:8) to humble themselves in God's sight so He would exalt them. God sees man's sinfulness and commands all men everywhere to repent (Luke 13:3, 5). God will restore those who have strayed that will come to him in humble submission and obedience.

To summarize what we have studied in verses 7-10, there are several commandments from God that James instructs a penitent believer to do to repent of doublemindedness: (1) submit oneself to God; (2) resist the devil; (3) draw nigh to God; (4) cleanse one's hands; (5) purify one's heart; (6) be afflicted; (7) mourn; (8) weep; (9) turn laughter into mourning; and (10) humble oneself in the sight of the Lord and he will lift the penitent up.

Lesson Nine Review Questions For Discussion (4: 4-10)

Verse 4

1. Who are the adulterers and adulteresses that James refers to in this verse? ____

2. Why are those who become a friend of the world the enemies of God? ____

3. How can a Christian commit spiritual adultery? ____

Verse 5

4. Must a Christian be on guard about allowing his/her inner person to envy or lust after the same evil things that carnal or worldly people possess? _____

_____

Verse 6

5. Explain how God's grace abounds more toward some than others. _____

_____

_____

6. How does God resist the proud? Who are the proud? _____

_____

_____

Verse 7

7. What does it mean to "resist the devil?" _____

_____

_____

Verse 8

8. How does a person draw near to God? _____

_____

Verse 9

9. Why is mourning a blessing (Matthew 5:4)? _____

_____

_____

Verse 10

10. How can a Christian draw nigh to God? _____

_____

_____

Lesson 10—James 4:11-17

⁓⁓⁓⁓⁓⁓⁓⁓⁓⁓⁓⁓⁓⁓ Commentary and Questions

4:11—Speak Not Evil One Of Another, Brethren

James addresses the "brethren" to stop speaking "evil one of another." The Greek word for "speak" is *katalaleo*, which is translated "to speak evil" (W.E. Vine's Dictionary). The evil speaking in this passage is that of unwarranted, derogatory remarks, such as slandering, criticizing, or exaggerating another brother's faults. It means to run another person down.

A believer who manifests love for his brethren should never speak evil against another member of the church. Rather than restoring those who overtaken in a fault, some choose to gossip or slander (Gal. 6:1-2). It is not uncommon to hear slandering, which can be characterized as mudslinging, backstabbing, and unjust criticism of others. This sin has prevailed in some local churches, although James directly forbids it in 3:15 as earthly, sensual, and devilish. Many Christians excuse evil-speaking by adding "bless his/her heart" before or after their words as if blessing another excuses sin. Ephesians 4:31-32 and 1 Peter 2:1 are just two examples where evil speaking is to be put aside or put away from everyone who professes to be an obedient believer of Jesus Christ. Knit-picking, mote-hunting, and speaking evil manifest an unloving attitude toward others.

He That Speaketh Evil Of His Brother

This part of the verse is probably referring to a fellow believer in Christ. It is unwise to speak against, slander, or run down another who is trying to serve the Lord. It is a sin against the perfect law of liberty to exercise the office of a self-appointed judge or censor and speak evil of a brother. "Speaking evil of his brother" abandons the law of love (James 2:8; Gal. 5:15). A child of God should refrain from speaking evil towards all men.

And Judgeth His Brother

No one has the right to judge another's motives. Only God knows the thoughts and intents of the heart. No one can look into another's heart and determine his/her motives for his/her actions. James is forbidding hypocritical judging that proceeds from sinful attitudes where one loves to find fault with others. Read Romans 14:10.

Jesus, our Lord, taught a valuable lesson about judging others with a rash and unjust judgment (Matt. 7:1-6). Never should one malign another or place the worst possible scenario on other people's words and actions. Unjust criticism is sinful. James is not condemning all forms of judging because there are times when one must confront a brother (Matt. 18:15-18; Rom. 16:17), or must make judgments when one is taking part in church discipline (1 Cor. 6:2-5), or must discern when a fellow believer is overtaken in a fault that needs to be corrected (Gal. 6:1-2). The writer of this letter is addressing unjust criticism that stems not from a love for God or his brother, but earthly wisdom (3:14-16). This criticism comes from envy, jealously, and selfish ambition.

Speaketh Evil Of The Law, And Judgeth The Law

For the Christian, James likely refers to the law of liberty or the law of Christ (1:25) and the royal law "Thou shalt love thy neighbor as thyself" (2:8). The mindset which thrives on finding fault among brethren is, in essence, judging or declaring God's divine law of loving his neighbor as being ineffective, worthless, or unimportant. Believers are not only to love God and His laws but also to love one another (1 John 4:7-8,11).

But If Thou Judge The Law,
Thou Art Not A Doer Of The Law, But A Judge

It is sinful for one to set oneself up as a critic or a censor of the law and of others rather than being a keeper of God's divine law. Possibly James is referring to the freedoms in the law of liberty when it comes to observances of O.T. ceremonial laws as did Paul in Colossians 2:16-18; Acts 15:10; Galatians 4:21-31.

Some of the brethren could have very well been speaking evil of others who were not observing some form of these Jewish rituals and therefore making judgments on the law of Christ (the perfect law of liberty). There is also that possibility of some who want to bind their personal faith on others as being the faith. Some may have set their standards or their private interpretation of Scriptures, thus binding others where Christ's laws have not bound. Our business as Christians is not to make laws or amend those that are made. Our responsibility is to keep the N.T. law of Christ that he has appointed. James commands the early disciples to be "doers" and not assume the office of "judges."

4:12—There Is One Lawgiver, Who Is Able To Save And To Destroy

There is only "one lawgiver" of the N.T. law and One Judge. God has given Him the preeminence over all things to the church (Col. 1:18; 2 John 9) and to be the Judge of all mankind (Rom. 14:10). Jesus Christ is that lawgiver and righteous Judge (2 Tim. 4:8) Who will judge us by His words (John 12:48). That same Lawgiver and Judge can save one with eternity in heaven or consign one to an eternity in hell. Read Matthew 10:28; Matt.hew 25:34, 41, 46; 2 Corinthians 5:10.

Who Art Thou That Judgeth Another

Stop it! Who are you that goes about judging others? Quit playing God! No one has the God-given right to judge another's motives or consign another person to heaven or hell. James is not saying that one cannot make a righteous judgment (John 7:24) should one see brothers or sisters practicing error. If one truly loves them, one will attempt to restore them in the spirit of meekness. But the "judges" James condemns are those self-appointed, egotistical, self-righteous, unloving judges. They are quick to speak in slandering other members of the church or wish to remove every blemish from others when they have beams sticking out of their own eyes (Matt. 7:3-5). Paul also warns Christians about condemning others or laying anything to the charge of God's elect whom He has justified (Rom. 8:33, 34).

4:13-15—Go To Now, Ye That Say, To Day Or To Morrow We Will Go Into Such A City, And Continue There A Year, And Buy And Sell, And Get Gain: (Vs. 14) Whereas Ye Know Not What Shall Be On The Morrow. For What Is Your Life? It Is Even A Vapour, That Appeareth For A Little Time, And Then Vanisheth Away. (Vs. 15) For That Ye Ought To Say, If The Lord Will, We Shall Live, And Do This, Or That

"Go to now, ye that say," James introduces a new subject that needed addressing among those who were scattered abroad. Some were confidently planning the future without considering the uncertainty of life and failing to include God's will in their plans. They said, "today or tomorrow we will go into such a city, and continue there a year, and buy and sell, and get gain." There was nothing wrong with these brethren carefully considering traveling into distant cities like Alexandra, Corinth, Antioch, and Ephesus seeking gainful employment. The wrong was that they fixed a definite time frame for when they would remain in a city, and when they would leave. They would buy and sell, make a profit, without relying upon God or first seeking His will.

It is not wrong to plan or set goals, but a child of God should never make plans for the future without absolute dependence upon God. James says, "Whereas ye know not what shall be on the morrow." Then he asks, "For what is your life? It is even a vapour, that appeareth for a little time, and then vanisheth away." They formed their plans as if they knew what tomorrow would bring. They did not consider what could occur, such as adversity or even death. There are uncertainties in life that often God's people fail to consider. No one knows the future but God himself. It seems that their planning was flawed because of a self-confident, self-dependent, and self-seeking spirit rather than dependency upon the Lord while setting their priorities.

There are two biblical examples where people leave God out of the picture. The first is a man in the O.T. by the name of "Asa" (2 Chron. 16:12-13) who was diseased in his feet and died because he sought help from the physicians but never sought the Lord. The second is the rich man in our Lord's parable who never once considered God in his plans, but said, "this will I do: I will pull down my barns, and will build greater; and there will I bestow all my fruits and my goods. And I will say to my soul, Soul thou hast much goods laid up for many years; take thine ease, eat, drink and be merry." Read Luke 12:16-21. But one can easily see that he didn't have God in any of his plans, and God said, "This night thy soul shall be required of thee." He was not rich toward God. James' readers were probably very familiar with these two examples.

James is teaching a valuable lesson for both the young and old. No one has the promise that one will even be alive the next minute, hour, day, week, month, or a year from now. It is folly for one to plan his future while leaving God out of his plans. The wise man admonishes, "Boast not thyself of tomorrow; for thou knowest not what a day may bring forth" (Proverbs 27:1). James is saying to consider life for it is like a fog or mist that appears for a little while but then vanishes away. He is reminding his readers that life is short, brief, and uncertain. I have talked with some older folks who lived to be nearly 100 years old, and they would always describe the brevity of their lives as being swift in passing. Believers and non-believers alike will often reply by asking, "Where has time gone?" Ofttimes I have made the statement, "My months have turned into weeks." Truly, when a Christian walks hand in hand with God, his/her life will seem to be swiftly passing. The brevity of life reminds us of the passage, which says, "But godliness with contentment is great gain" (1 Tim. 6:6). The psalmist declares that "we spend our years as a tale that is told" (Psa. 90:9). Psalm 37:18 says, "The Lord knoweth the days of the upright: and their inheritance shall be forever." The lesson of James is simple and straight to the point: always trust in God and include Him in all your plans because life is short, and no one knows when he/she will draw that last breath.

James now states the right attitude towards God and life: "Ye ought to say, if the Lord will, we shall live, and do this, or that." One should never boast of what his/her plans are without having the proper attitude of doing God's will first and foremost. One should never leave God out of their choices, whatever goals, dreams, or plans for the future they make.

Pray and seek God's guidance that He will open those doors of opportunity and blessing. The Apostle Paul often uses the same or a similar phrase, including God in his plans (Acts 18:21, 1 Cor. 4:19, 16:7 and Heb. 6:3). Every child of God should include God in their plans, whether he reasons to himself or says it verbally to others to show his/her dependency upon the Lord. It is certainly proper to say if it be the Lord's will but not as an empty phrase on one's lips without a sincere trust in God to direct one's paths in the future. Read the following comparable verses found in Psalm 37:23-24; Proverbs 16:7-9; Jeremiah 10:23.

4:16—But Now Ye Rejoice In Your Boastings: All Such Rejoicing Is Evil

Proverbs 27:1 says, "Boast not thyself of tomorrow; for thou knowest not what a day shall bring forth." Such a person who is so self-reliant in his plans for the future is looked upon as one who is boastful; one who rejoices in his decision-making without first seeking God's help is not wise. Those who were guilty of rejoicing in their "boastings" were those who were confident in their skills, abilities, and successes. Some of these brethren were doing so without any reference to God or His will. James says that "all such rejoicing is evil." Young Christians today should plan to find the right Christian mate, plan a family, or future employment, but not without first seeking His approval and blessing. Those who were boasting in verses 13-16 were doing so without any reference to God's will. All should pray as Jesus said, "Thy will be done" (Matt. 6:10).

417—Therefore To Him That Knoweth To Do Good, And Doeth It Not, To Him It Is Sin

"Therefore" probably has reference to the point specified in verses 13-16 of a believer recklessly forming plans for the future without first seeking God's approval because of the uncertainty of even being alive tomorrow. A wise person will ask God to open the doors of opportunity, according to His Divine will. Knowing one's dependency on God is good. Seeking God's will before making decisions about the future is good. When one fails to seek God's approval first before making their plans, it is a sin of omission.

Some Bible students understand that verse 17 is referring to all of James' instructions in the previous chapters of this epistle. Others believe it is a principle set forth in all of the Bible. Certainly, the failure to do anything that one knows to be good is plain, downright sin (Gr. *harmartia*), meaning to miss the mark concerning the will of God (1 John 3:4). The sin of omission can also be the result of putting things off, slothfulness, or deferring those things one knows to be good. Read Matthew 25:31-46; Galatians 6:2, 9-10. The greatest danger threatening a Christian's spiritual welfare is probably not the sins of commission like stealing, drunkenness, or adultery, but the sin of omission to the point that one's spiritual life is devoid of good works and doing God's righteousness. Remember, it is sinful to know what one ought to do and then not do it.

Lesson 10 Review Questions For Discussion (4:11-17)

Verse 11
1. How does God view slander, running another brother down and mudslinging?

_____

_____

James ————————————————————————

Verse 12

2. Who is the judge of all mankind that is able to save or destroy? _____

3. Why is judging (other than righteous judgment) wrong? ————————————
_____

_____

Vv. 13-15

4. What type of setting goals would be wrong for a Christian? Why? _____
_____

5. Give an illustration from the Scriptures:

   a. which shows how one should not approach future event/plans - _____
_____

   b. which shows how one should approach future events/plans - _____
_____

Verse 16

6. Why is boasting about the future evil? _____
_____

_____

Verse 17

7. How is sin defined in this verse? _____
_____

8. Serving God by removing sin is only part of one's responsibilites. What else is necessary (Consider Luke 11:24-26)? ————————————————————
_____

_____

Chapter 5

~~~~~~~~~~~~~~~~~~~Analysis and Brief Summary

Vss. 1-2
James explains the source of conflicts, wars, and dissensions. Division can be traced to the "lust" of men.

Verse 3
James deals with praying without proper motives.

Verse 4
Discusses how the desire of this world is enmity with God.

Verse 5- 6
Deals with envy as the result of lust in one's heart and God resists all those who are proud and gives grace to all of them who manifest humbleness (verse 6).

Vss. 7-10
Teaches that friendship with God is the solution to these problems.

Vss. 11-12
Jame issues warnings against speaking evil or defaming our brethren by playing God and becoming a judge. There is only one lawgiver.

Vss. 13-17
Christians must depend upon God's will because man's life upon earth swiftly passes. Leaving God out of one's plans is evil; therefore, to him, that knows to do good and does it not, it is a sin.

Lesson 11—James 5:1-12

5:1—Go To Now, Ye Rich Men, Weep And Howl For Your Miseries That Shall Come Upon You

The ASV says, "Come now." James uses this expression to attract attention, as he did in 4:13. He wants the rich to listen and take heed to what he says next. These are the wealthy who had acquired great riches by fraudulent means mentioned in the next few verses. James condemns the manner of life of the ungodly rich (verses 1-6). James does not use the word "brethren" in the first six verses, so it is impossible to say with certainty whether he is addressing unbelieving Jews or those who were once believers that had gone astray. The condemnation of the rich in these verses is not that some had material wealth, but how they obtained their wealth and how they were oppressing the poor. Whether they were believers or non-believers, all Bible students agree that covetousness is idolatry (Col. 3:5) that dethrones God from one's heart.

Paul tells Timothy to flee those lusts that can end up causing him much grief, one of which is the love of money. "But they that will be rich fall into temptation and a snare, and into many foolish and hurtful lusts, which can drown men in destruction and perdition. For the love of money is the root of all evil: which while some coveted after, they have erred from the faith, and pierced themselves through with many sorrows" (1 Tim. 6:9-10). Every sort of wickedness and vice, in one way or another, stems from the root of one's love of money, which could result in total and utter ruin.

"Weep and howl for your miseries that shall come upon you" is a severe warning to these rich oppressors. "Weep" (Gr. klaio) "which is any loud expression of grief," while "howl" in this verse (ololuzo) is "in an exhortation to the godless rich" (W.E. Vines Dictionary). James is using these words to warn the ungodly rich of their forthcoming misery and God's judgment that is coming upon them because of their ill-gotten gains, especially from robbing the poor. Here in this passage, James uses weep and howl in the sense of despair. One can find similar words are used in the O.T. when God's judgment descended upon foreign nations (Isa. 13:6; 14:31). "For your miseries that shall come upon you" probably is a warning to all ungodly rich oppressors of the poor that they have exposed themselves to the coming wrath of God. James alluded to hell (3:2), and he speaks of the "coming of the Lord" (5:7). These warnings should remind Christians today of the deceitfulness of riches and the judgment that unjust gain can bring upon them.

There are several scriptural ways one can obtain legitimate money: (1) earn it the old-fashion way by working for it (Eph. 4:28); (2) receiving an inheritance; (3) receiving a gift; (4) or getting gain through some honest business. Although one may become wealthy through legitimate means, one must never allow covetousness to rule one's life by wanting more and more. Jesus said, "Take heed and beware of covetousness: for man's life consisteth not in the abundance of the things which he possesseth (Luke 12:15). Some of God's choicest saints in the O.T. were wealthy. The Lord prospered men like Abraham, Job, David, and Solomon but the condemnation by James was not because one becomes wealthy, but how one obtains and uses that wealth.

5:2 Your Riches Are Corrupted, And Your Garments Are Motheaten. 5:3 Your Gold And Silver Is Cankered; And The Rust Of Them Shall Be A Witness Against You, And Shall Eat Your Flesh As It Were Fire

When James says, "your riches are corrupted," he means the ill-gotten gains they have obtained are rotten and useless. Their fine clothing is becoming similar to what the rich man owned in our Lord's narrative (Luke 16:19); his attire was of purple and fine linen (kingly attire). They were storing these garments, which moths would eventually destroy rather than putting their garments to good use. James possibly could have been making a connection with fine clothing in 2:2 and "motheaten" garments in this verse. Your money and precious valuables are "cankered" or corroded like an eating sore that spreads with gangrene. "Rust" is used metaphorically as their riches are lying stored and useless, just like their clothes. Their wealth from ill-gotten gains will be of no value, "and the rust of them shall be a witness against you and shall eat your flesh as it were fire." Rust not only destroys the riches stored up by these ungodly men, but figuratively, these riches will also destroy them like a fire that consumes flesh. Some commentators apply this part of the verse to the coming destruction of Jerusalem and the state of everlasting separation from God. Read Matthew 5:22, 29, 30; 10:28. Although the Scriptures speak of the destruction of Jerusalem, one cannot say with certainty that this verse is speaking of that event that came about in about A.D. 70.

Ye Have Heaped Treasure Together For The Last Days.

They had stored up treasure for "the last days." The ASV renders this part of this verse, "Ye have laid up your treasure in the last days." The expression "last days" could have several meanings, but it is my understanding that it means the last days of this dispensation. This age or dispensation started on the day of Pentecost and will last until the second coming of Christ or the end of time. Other inspired writers of the N.T. also refer to the last days (Acts 2:17; Heb. 1:1-2). My understanding of this part of the passage is that "the last days" are the days of grace, the time and opportunity God has given us to lay up treasures in heaven. Jesus said to His disciples, "Lay not up for yourselves treasures upon the earth, where moth and rust doth corrupt, and where thieves break through and steal: But lay up for yourselves treasures in heaven" (Matt. 6:19-20). The wicked rich of James' day were ignoring the will of God by laying up treasures for themselves only on the earth and by doing so were depriving themselves of any hope of heaven. So this is what Christians can learn from these first three verses of this chapter: hoarding of riches will result in waste and spoilage, which will witness against them in the day of judgment. Greediness and selfishness will result in condemnation to those who are found guilty on that day. Paul writes, "But after thy hardness and impenitent heart treasurest up unto thyself wrath against the day of wrath and revelation of the righteous judgment of God; Who will render to every man according to his deeds" (Rom. 2:5-6). Read with understanding what Jesus said about laying up treasures in Matthew 6:19-21.

5:4—Behold, The Hire Of Your Labourers Who Have Reaped Down Your Fields, Which Is Of You Kept Back By Fraud, Crieth: And The Cries Of Them Which Have Reaped Are Entered Into The Ears Of The Lord Of Sabaoth

The rich landowners who had hired the poor workers to harvest their fields had defrauded or cheated them of their rightfully earned wages. No doubt, these defrauded workers were crying unto the Lord of Sabaoth or the Lord of hosts (Psa. 24:10). The cries of the poor come up to the ears of the Lord as did the blood of Abel from the ground after Cain had slain his brother (Gen. 4:10). The point Christians should gather from these scriptures is that God sees all wrongdoing, and nothing goes unnoticed because fraud cries out before God. He will take note of the injustices of the rich towards the poor; these defrauders will receive the proper judgment. In the O.T., God commanded the laborer to be paid every day after his workday. The worker should receive a fair price for a fair day of labor. Read Proverbs 22:22-23; Proverbs 17:5; and Psalm 9:9.

Today it should also be considered unjust for an employee or an employer to defraud one another. In the 21st century, wicked rich politicians, various pharmaceutical companies, and other industrialized manufacturer defraud the common laborer, the consumers, and the taxpayers. One can rest assured the fraud that one is witnessing by corporate greed does not go unnoticed by the God of heaven. Although the rich may perpetrate fraudulent schemes against the poor or working class, there is a day of reckoning coming when all involved will receive a just recompense for their evil deeds.

5:5—Ye Have Lived In Pleasure On The Earth, And Been Wanton

Pleasure and wantonness describes the lifestyle of some of the rich and famous then as well as today. Their god is pleasure-seeking all the days of their lives. They seem to live for the moment, grabbing all the gusto, food, fun, and frolic that is available. They reason in their minds that whatever makes them happy, they should do because one only goes around once in this life, so eat, drink, and be merry. Never once do they consider they are accountable before God. This lifestyle seems to be the object of most Hollywood movie stars who live lives of lascivious, lewd, and lustful pleasures with no sense of the forthcoming judgment of God. James is not saying that one cannot enjoy some leisure, rest, and relaxation in this life, but he does warn against those who are always seeking wanton pleasure as a lifestyle. Read with understanding 1 Timothy 6:17-19.

Ye Have Nourished Your Hearts, As In A Day Of Slaugter

James uses an analogy of cattle, sheep, fatted fowl, or some other eatable live-stock that will gorge themselves, not realizing their day of slaughter is drawing near. Likewise, the rich and wealthy are fattening their hearts by living in pleasure and never looking to their future destiny. They are like the proverbial hog eating acorns under the tree and never look up to see from where the blessings are coming. "The day of slaughter" is probably the day of judgment that is to come.

5:6—Ye Have Condemned And Killed The Just; And He Doth Not Resist You

James denounced the rich in verses 2-5 for misusing their wealth and abusing the poor. Now, in vs.6, he continues to address some of the ungodly rich who would condemn the just in courts of law even unto the killing of the just. It appears that James is speaking of judicial murder. The wicked rich of James' day would often bring the poor before the courts and tribunals and use their power and influence to oppress these victims, even unto death. "And he doth not resist you" means the poor had no recourse against their oppressors in the courts of law. Like the defrauded laborers whose wages the ungodly rich had taken, these just ones had no one to plead their cause. The poor probably had no other choice but to submit to these unjust verdicts and even the death that often faced them.

5:7—Be Patient Therefore, Brethren

Some of the poor brethren had been put to death (v. 6). because of the power and influence of rich oppressors, but the writer encourages others, "Be patient." James admonishes his fellow believers to endure these afflictions because the Lord will, in His own time, bring judgment upon their oppressors. The word "therefore" in this verse seems to suggest the writer is concluding what was said in verses 1-6 about the persecution of the righteous poor at the hands of the ungodly rich.

The doctrine of Christ in the N.T. instructs Christians to practice patience in their daily godly living. The word "patient" (Gr. hupo-under, meno-to abide) therefore means an abiding under; in 5:7 the meaning of patience is from the Greek word makrothumesate (makrothumeo) literally means to be long suffering or to patiently hold up under sufferings (see W.E. Vine's Dictionary). These poor oppressed saints are to suffer long the wrongs committed against them. In 1:3, James introduces patience when he informed the brethren that "the trying of your faith worketh patience." Patience is a trait of character that Peter commands all Christians to add to their faith with all diligence (2 Peter 1:5-7). Trials, persecutions, and afflictions in this life can be profitable because "tribulation worketh patience" (Rom. 5:3).

Unto The Coming Of The Lord

Bible students and commentators have various opinions as to which future judgment James refers. Some think James is referring to the destruction of Jerusalem which was drawing nigh, while others lean toward the second coming of Christ where He will judge the world at that event by passing judgment on the ungodly and casting them into the lake of fire which is the second death (Rev. 20:12-15). Exactly when God will bring judgment upon these rich oppressors and give them what they justly deserve is in the hands of the Almighty. We cannot say with certainty to which judgment James is referencing because similar language in the Scriptures describes both the destruction of Jerusalem and the Lord's second coming. This verse is probably relating to Christ's second coming because it fits the context and the remaining verses of this chapter.

Behold, The Husbandman Waiteth For The Precious Fruit Of The Earth, And Hath Long Patience For It, Until He Receive The Early And Latter Rain

An example of one who practices patience is the husbandman or farmer. He plows the ground and sows the seed. The farmer does his part, and then he patiently waits upon God to do His part by sending the sunshine and the rain to make his crops grow. The farmer thus has "long patience" for the bountiful harvest. James is admonishing the suffering brethren to patiently wait upon the Lord to bring judgment upon their rich oppressors, just as the farmer patiently waits for his harvest.

5:8—Be Ye Also Patient; Stablish Your Hearts: For The Coming Of The Lord Draweth Nigh

"Be ye also patient" as the husbandman in verse 7 who patiently waits for the early and the latter rains. "Stablish your hearts" means to strengthen your hearts and not grow "weary in well doing" (Gal. 6:9). They are to keep their faith firm and unwavering because "the coming of the Lord draweth nigh." The N.T. Scriptures speak of the coming of the Lord as being at hand, coming quickly, or drawing nigh. All inspired writers talk about this advent as being near or imply it is soon to occur. The Lord could return at any moment.

5:9 Grudge Not One Against Another, Brethren, Lest Ye Be Condemned: Behold, The Judge Standeth Before The Door

In addition to patiently waiting on the Lord to bring forth judgment on the wicked, James instructs the brethren, "grudge not one against another." In other words, don't complain or grumble against each other, "lest ye be condemned." The "judge standeth before the door" means the Lord is approaching the door or standing before the door to soon come in judgment. The KJV uses the word "grudge," while the ASV uses the word "murmur," signifying to groan or grumble. Some brethren ofttimes manifest an attitude of dissatisfaction or discontentment toward those who have prospered more than themselves. Murmuring will bring the Lord's condemnation. It also could mean that obedient believers are not to complain and murmur because the Lord doesn't react immediately according to their timetable. When ungodly people persecute believers, they persecute God. He does not always bring immediate judgment; however, nothing goes unnoticed by the Lord who sees all.

5:10—Take, My Brethren, The Prophets, Who Have Spoken In The Name Of The Lord, For An Example Of Suffering Affliction, And Of Patience

Another example of suffering and patience is "the prophets," of which the early church was familiar. They exercised "patience" while under persecution (Acts 7:52; Heb. 11:37-38). The prophets were stoned, sawn asunder, slain with the sword, made destitute, afflicted, tormented, and made to wander in deserts, mountains, and dens and caves of the earth. Yet, they manifested the proper attitude of suffering for their faith and continued to speak in the name of the Lord, even to the point of death. These men of God are good examples of suffering and patience while speaking in the name of the Lord.

5:11—Behold, We Count Them Happy Which Endure. Ye Have Heard Of The Patience Of Job, And Have Seen The End Of The Lord; That The Lord Is Very Pitiful, And Of Tender Mercy

The ASV reads, "Behold, we call them blessed that endured." Christians today, as well as believers in the first century, can be counted "happy" when bearing up under the trials and afflictions of life while remaining faithful, as did the prophets. Read comparable verses in 1:2, Matthew 5:11-12; and 1 Peter 3:14; 4:14. W.E. Vine's dictionary defines "endured" from the Greek word *hupomenontas* (*hupomeno*) as meaning "to abide under, to bear up courageously (under suffering)."

James now gives a third example of practicing patience and endurance. His readers would have been familiar with Job and his patience, longsuffering, and perseverance. Job endured the loss of his wealth and possessions (Job 1:13-17), loss of his children (Job 1:18-19), loss of his physical health (Job 2:7-8), and at one point, the loss of his wife's support (Job 2:9). "Have seen the end of the Lord; that the Lord is very pitiful, and of tender mercy" seems to be referring to the end of the book of Job, which records the outcome of Job's patience. God blesses him with twice the amount of riches in the end than he had at the beginning (Job 42:12-17). The Lord was "pitiful and of tender mercy" towards Job, whose patience was shaken by the things he suffered at the beginning, and he seemingly questioned the ways of God but later repented. However, Job never gave up his faith but persevered through all his trials and received God's blessings in the end. James wanted to point out to his readers that God will bless all His faithful saints who endure life's afflictions and hardships, who practice patience, and who do not lose faith.

5:12—But Above All Things, My Brethren, Swear Not, Neither By Heaven, Neither By The Earth, Neither By Any Other Oath: But Let Your Yea Be Yea; And Your Nay, Nay; Lest Ye Fall Into Condemnation

"But above all things" is an expression used by James to warn early disciples concerning swearing, taking vows, or any other oath using God's name or His creation. He probably is reminding his Jewish brethren of God's law, which says: "And ye shall not swear by my name falsely, neither shalt thou profane the name of thy God: I am the Lord (Lev. 19:12). Also, "When thou shalt vow a vow unto the Lord thy God, thou shalt not slack to pay it: for the Lord thy God shall require it of thee; and it would be sin in thee. But if thou shalt forbear, it shall be no sin in thee. That which is gone out of thy lips thou shalt keep and perform; even a free will offering, according as thou hast vowed unto the Lord thy God, which thou hast promised with thy mouth" (Deut. 23:21-23). James repeats in substance what Jesus said in Matthew 5:33-36. He is simply telling them not to swear by heaven for it is God's throne, by the earth for it is His footstool, neither by Jerusalem, for it is the city of the great King.

Followers of Christ should not swear in their daily conversations with others to put greater emphasis on what they are about to say. A simple yes or no is all that is needed among followers of Christ. "Lest you fall into condemnation" or as our Lord said, "But let your communication be Yea, yea; Nay, nay; for whatsoever is more than these cometh of evil" (Matt. 5:37). Swearing is just another instance of what James talked about in chapter 3 concerning sins of the tongue and the principle of being "slow to speak" (1:19). James warns against invoking God's name, needlessly, to guarantee one's truthfulness.

The question arises then, is it sinful to take an oath? There may arise certain situations where one must give testimony in courts of law where one has been summonsed and asked to swear or affirm that one's testimony will be the truth, the whole truth, nothing but the truth, so help me God. In our courts of law today, one can reply, "I affirm" for conscience's sake. Most courts today allow people to affirm (to state as a fact) that what they are about to say is true. Should any Christian today take an oath, affirm or swear before God, he/she is calling upon the Lord to be a witness that he/she is telling the truth; therefore, he/she will be subject to His condemnation if untruthful. God took oaths in the O.T. and required keeping

James

oaths even to the point of death. In the N.T., God took an oath (Heb. 6:17-18), Jesus took an oath (Matt. 26:63-64; Mark 14:61-62) as he stood before the Sanhedrin court, and Paul took oaths (Rom. 1:9). So, we know it is not a sin to take an oath under certain circumstances. It seems that James, in this passage, is talking about taking frivolous oaths while having ordinary conversations with others. Every Christian must be 100% truthful at all times because one's word is one's bond.

Lesson Eleven Review Questions For Discussion (5: 1-12)

Verse 1

1. How can one know it is not sinful to be wealthy? _____
_____
_____

2. How is the love of money the root of all evil and drowns one in destruction and perdition? _____
_____
_____

Verse 2 and 3

3. Identify the dangers of storing up earthly riches. _____
_____
_____

Verse 4

4. How can an employer as well as an employee defraud one another? _____
_____
_____

Verse 5

5. What is "wanton pleasure?" _____
_____

6. To what could "the day of slaughter" be referring? _____
_____

Verse 6

7. What is judicial murder? _____
_____
_____

8. What can be learned from the Lord's death regarding those guilty of judicial murder (Acts 2:23, 36; 3:14-15)? _____

_____

Verse 7.

9. Identify at least two things a suffering Christian can learn from the patience of a farmer. _____

_____

_____

Verse 8

10. What does it mean to "stablish you your hearts?" _____

_____

_____

Verse 9

11. Why is it wrong to complain, grumble, or murmur against our brethren? __

_____

_____

Verse 10

12. Considering the treatment of the prophest of God and their patience (Heb. 11:37-38), how can one demonstrate patience today? _____

_____

_____

Verse 11

12. Considering the end results of the patience of the farmer, the prophets, and Job, what is the end result of a Christian's patience today? _____

_____

_____

Verse 12.

13. What is and is not included in James' warning for Christians to "swear not," "neither by any other oath?" _____

_____

_____

_____

Lesson 12—James 5:13-20

Commentary and Questions

5:13—Is Any Among You Afflicted? Let Him Pray

James has discussed persecution, trials, and afflictions throughout this epistle and now continues to encourage the brethren concerning the power of prayer during these trying times. He offers the remedy for all suffering believers who are patiently enduring torments or hardships of any kind to pray. God's remedy for the one suffering is to "let him pray." Whether the suffering is physical, mental, or spiritual, the antidote for the individual is to pray in these troublesome times. "Pray without ceasing" is commanded in 1 Thessalonians 5:17.

Prayer brings each one strength from God in times of need. The obedient believer has the freedom and privilege to call upon the Almighty God 24/7 because our Lord is ready, willing, and able to hear and relieve or give strength to one in all of life's afflictions. Jesus taught His disciples to pray private prayers, "enter into thy closet, and when thou hast shut the door, pray to thy Father which is in secret; and thy Father which seeth in secret shall reward thee openly" (Matt. 6:6). God is there to help, but one must "come boldly unto the throne of grace, that we may obtain mercy, and find grace to help in time of need" (Heb. 4:16). A faithful child of God will take his burdens to the Lord and leave them there. Peter says, "Casting all your care upon him; for he careth for you" (1 Peter 5:7). David, a man after God's own heart, either writes or compiles, "God is our refuge and strength, a very present help in trouble (Psa. 46:1)." Prayer brings strength in all of life's difficulties, sufferings, and affliction. Jesus taught His faithful disciples to ask, seek, and knock on heaven's door in all circumstances when facing life's uneven ways (Matt. 7:7-8). Romans 8:31 reminds Christians, "If God be for us, who can be against us?"

Read an O.T. example of the power of prayer when God's people take their burdens to the Lord and leaves them in his hands (Isa. 37:14-36). When Hezekiah realized the Assyrians were about to slay all of them, he took the matter before God by spreading the letter before the Lord and praying for God's intervention. Can you imagine what went through the minds of God's people as they looked out and viewed 185,000 corpses of their enemies, and not one of God's people had so much as to lift his sword? Can we truly say, "God is my refuge and strength"?

109

Is Any Merry? Let Him Sing Psalms

To make or be "merry" in the N.T. Scriptures means pleasant, agreeable, and free from troubles. A Christian glorifies God when praying during affliction or singing praises when happy, cheerful, or blessed. Singing praises or praying unto God is not limited to just the worship assemblies of the church, but one can praise Him by singing psalms at any time, especially when one's heart is joyous, happy, and thankful. James seems to be teaching communication with God. If one is afflicted, one should pray. If one is merry, one should sing praises unto God. One should approach God in either circumstance. Remember, Paul and Silas were beaten with many stripes and were cast into the inner prison with their feet in stocks, yet they could be heard at midnight praying and singing praises unto God (Acts 16:22-25).

5:14—Is Any Sick Among You? Let Him Call For The Elders Of The Church; And Let Them Pray Over Him, Anointing Him With Oil In The Name Of The Lord

In the previous verse, James talks about daily afflictions and how one is to pray for oneself according to God's remedy. Now, in verse 14, he seems to address the physically sick. He continues to set forth the power of prayer as in the previous verses. Many times, in the first century, members of the church had to deal with mental affliction and physical and spiritual sickness. The Greek word (*astheneo*) is translated sick, which literally means to be weak, feeble, or without strength and is a term often used for physical illness. The context of James 5:14 seems to be that of physical sickness.

When these illnesses occur, God offers a remedy that is still effective in one's treatment or recovery. There is a pattern that should be followed: first, the offering of prayers by the elders for one who is sick, and then "anointing him with oil" as a means of aiding, relieving, or refreshing the sick person. God has placed the responsibility on the sick person to contact the elders because they are not mindful of everyone in the congregation who is sick. The elders praying at the bedside of the physically sick and beseeching God's favor to bring about healing is first and foremost. Sometimes the sick person may not have the mindset because of his sickness to pray for himself, but the elders praying with him and for him wording the prayer of faith is of utmost importance should it be the Lord's will that the sick person recover.

Now, why send for the elders of the local church? Why not the deacons, preachers, evangelists, or the most spiritual ones of the church? There are many reasons why we can understand God's instruction to send for the elders of the church. Who would better know the physical and spiritual condition of one in the flock over which God has given them the responsibility to oversee (Acts 20:28)? The qualified elders are men of the congregation who are knowledgeable and concerned about those who are under their oversight. The elders have this God-given responsibility and must one day give an account (Heb. 13:17). They are qualified men (1 Tim. 3:1-7) and are willing to take the oversight and feed the flock among them (1 Peter 5:1-4). This office over which the Holy Ghost has made them overseers is the office that God ordained to carry out this special work. Qualified men who hold this office in a local congregation are referred to in the N.T. as bishops, overseers, shepherds, and elders. The Divine arrangement seen throughout the N.T. is for a plurality of these men to be appointed in each local church. I ask then, who could be better qualified to offer an effectual fervent prayer over the physically sick than these qualified elders? They are mature, spiritually qualified men (Titus 1:5-9) to whom God has appointed and given this responsibility. They should know each member of the flock and his/her needs, both physically and spiritually.

Some commentators believe James is speaking of elders who were endowed with miraculous gifts. It is a possibility that some of these elders of the early church could have possessed miraculous gifts (1 Cor. 12:28). However, James does not specifically address the elders who possessed miraculous gifts, but he addresses all elders in general. There is no indication in the Scriptures that all elders had these gifts like Jesus or the apostles. This admonishment for the elders of the church to be called would be those who would hold this office even after miraculous gifts were to cease (see 1 Cor. 13:8-13).

It is not my intent to list all the many ways that the word "anointing" is used in the Scriptures nor to attempt to point out every false doctrine that practices the misuse of the text. My interest is to properly understand the text and give the context of these verses. James 5:14 uses the Greek word *aleipho*, which is the verb form meaning the physical refreshment after the washing of the sick (W.E. Vine's Dictionary of N.T. Words). However, the Scriptures do not tell us the kind of oil used. So, after reading the text, James seems to be referring to praying for the sick, anointing with oil to aid or refresh after washing while relieving the afflicted. The elders are not medical doctors, but they can use any appropriate means at their disposal to aid or relieve the suffering of the sick person while praying by faith. In another instance, Jesus referred to using oil for purposes of treating wounds (Luke 10:34). So, the anointing of oil used in James 5:14 seems to be for purposes of aiding and refreshing of the physically sick in one's recovery. Man can treat or aid the sufferings of others, but only God can heal.

"In the name of the Lord" means by the authority of the Lord or following His directions or instructions. Any act of obedience to God's commandments can be said to be in His name. The acts of praying for the sick, refreshing the physically sick, or aiding the afflictions of others certainly meets God's approval. "In the name of the Lord" and "in My name" can be found many times in the N.T. Scriptures. Read just a few: Matthew 18:5, 20; 19:29; 24:9; Mark 9:41; Luke 21:12, 17; Colossians 3:17; Revelation 2:3.

The examples of aiding the bedridden saints are many in my lifetime. I have seen my earthly father go to the bedside of the sick to wash and groom the sick by cutting the hair, shaving, and refreshing the sick after praying for them. Also, I have seen faithful sisters in the church administer aid to bedridden sisters in their homes back before modern methods were available. These faithful sisters, including my mother, would wash, clean, change clothing, and administer aid in any manner possible. 1 Timothy 5:10 lists several good works approved by God that a Christian woman can do in the home for "relieving the afflicted." These faithful saints will not lose their reward. Relieving the afflictions and suffering of fellow saints is a good work which does not go unnoticed by the Lord. See Jesus' instructions in Matthew 25:34-40. In modern times, there are more ways and means of treating the sick. There are medicines, doctors, and health care facilities that are available that were not available in James' day. We should always remember, God's part and man's part are needed together in taking care of the sick. Healing is in the hands of God. Faith and work are man's part (James 2:24). Remember Asa (2 Chron. 16:12-13). His legacy is that he left God out of the picture by consulting the physicians only, and he died. Doctors can offer treatments, but only God can heal. Any Bible student who studies the Scriptures will never deny the divine healing of the Almighty God. It is the "prayer of faith" that saves the sick in the next verse, and who could better pray this prayer than the elders?

5:15—And The Prayer Of Faith Shall Save The Sick, And The Lord Shall Raise Him Up

The "prayer of faith" is what "shall save the sick," that is, a prayer that shows confidence in God. Prayer saves the sick rather than the anointing of oil. Who could better pray this prayer than the elders? It is probable that some had grown weary and had become weak. It is hard to determine whether James is addressing a spiritual sickness or physical sickness in this verse. In either case, "the Lord shall raise him up" is an act of the Lord. He is "able to do exceeding abundantly above all that we ask or think" (Eph. 3:20).

Every child of God needs to learn how to pray a prayer of faith eventually. The teaching of James in these verses is to show the effectiveness or the power of prayer. God hears the prayers of His righteous servants (elders) who pray the prayer of faith, thus praying with confidence that God will answer. "And this is the confidence that we have in Him, that, if we ask any thing according to His will, He heareth us" (1 John 5:14). "The prayer of faith" must also include praying according to the Lord's will. According to the Lord's will refers to the authority of God Who gave instructions to the shepherds of a local congregation to oversee the flock among them and go when called upon to pray a confident prayer of faith without doubting. Neither the Bible nor this passage teaches one not to use medicines, see a doctor, or have surgery when needed, but the early believers would have used home remedies for treatments. The healing was a result of the elders praying the "prayer of faith" over the sick and "the Lord shall raise him up."

This passage affirms that all healing ultimately depends upon the will of God. The Lord, through His divine healing, will restore the sick if it is according to His will. God could restore and bring about the healing of the sick in the first-century church just as He does today. Although some in the early church had the gift of healing, miracles had divine purposes that were ordained by God. Men of God, like Paul and Timothy, suffered physical infirmities but never depended on the exercise of miraculous gifts for their healing. Miracles, signs, and wonders were to confirm that the messenger/message was from God.

And If He Have Committed Sins, They Shall Be Forgiven Him

"If" he has committed sins, the elders could pray for a penitent person whose physical sickness may or may not be the result of his sins. The physically sick, as well as the spiritual restoration, can be recognized here in this verse. The point again is to express the importance of praying the "prayer of faith," which is like lancing a festering boil when the elders pray for the sick and the afflicted. If the sick person has strayed, then he could be restored to the fold. In any case, the elders of the local church should know the physical and spiritual needs of every individual who is a member of that flock over which they are to oversee.

5:16—Confess Your Faults One To Another, And Pray One For Another, That Ye May Be Healed

The ASV says, "Confess therefore your sins one to another, and pray one for another, that ye may be healed." The KJV renders the Greek word *parapto-ma* as "faults," while the ASV renders the same word as "sins." The meaning of the Koine reads ta paraptoma, which means a false step, a trespass (W.E. Vine's Dictionary). What one is to confess means faults, sins, or transgressions.

There are two interpretations of this verse. One is that James is beginning a new thought in verse 16, where he says, "confess your faults one to another, and pray one for another." The other is to "confess therefore your sins" against God, and have mutual prayer one for another. The word "therefore" is found in some translations, which could reflect a continuation of verse 15. James could be referring to the sick in the previous verse, or he could also be referring to all obedient believers then and Christians now who know the value of mutual intercessory prayer one for another.

Confessing our faults one to another and praying one for another brings about healing. James refers to "sins" in the previous verse and "faults" in this verse. Both words could be referring to the same transgressing of God's law or could be referring to a guilty conscience because one is lacking in some respect because of one's weaknesses and shortcomings. Faults could also apply to conflicts between members of the church who, by mutual confession and praying one for another, could resolve any differences that may arise. Again, the teaching of James in these verses shows the effectiveness or the power of prayer.

The Effectual Fervent Prayer Of A Righteous Man Availeth Much

"The supplication of a righteous man availeth much in its working" (ASV). Prayers and supplications are requests we make known by earnestly entreating God for His favor (1 Tim. 2:1). A righteous man's prayer that is "effectual" is one that is appropriate and fitting. If there is anything that can prevail with God, it is a fervent prayer of a just person who is petitioning God for His divine favor. This kind of prayer is effective in obtaining blessings, and it accomplishes much when He answers.

Jesus said, "Ask, and it shall be given you; seek, and ye shall find; knock, and it shall be opened unto you" (Matt. 7:7). "Of a righteous man" is one who has been cleansed and justified by the blood of Jesus; he is just in his doings and character and is practicing God's righteousness in his daily walks of life (John 9:31). Thus, this kind of prayer can prevail with God, and it gets God's much-needed attention that produces action on God's part.

5:17—Elias Was A Man Subject To Like Passions As We Are, And He Prayed Earnestly That It Might Not Rain; And It Rained Not On The Earth By The Space Of Three Years And Six Months

Although Elias or Elijah was a prophet of God, he still was a man of prayer. He prayed with passion just as believers prayed in James's day, and Christians do today. Prayer was essential for Elijah as it was for Christ, who prayed for things that could be accomplished only by prayer. James says Elijah was a man of "like passions as we are," meaning he had the same kind of feelings, endured the same type of hardships, and shared similar life experiences as believers do today. He prayed earnestly, and God withheld rain from the earth three and a half years (See 1 Kings 17:1; 18:41-45). So, one could understand this to mean that one is to pray with such "like passions" as Elias. God can and does hear the prayers of the righteous, and yes, He hears the effectual fervent prayers of the righteous when praying for the sick and restores them (5:15). "And this is the confidence that we have in him, that, if we ask any thing according to his will, he heareth us: And if we know that he hear us, whatsoever we ask, we know that we have the petitions that we desired of him" (1 John 5:14-15).

5:18—And He Prayed Again, And The Heaven Gave Rain, And The Earth Brought Forth Her Fruit

James said, "And he prayed again, and the heaven gave rain." As you read 1 Kings 18:41, 42, you see Elijah putting his head down between his knees, and although the O.T. account doesn't specifically say he was praying, James says he was. "The heaven was black with clouds and wind, and there was a great rain" (v. 45). The famine ceased, and land produced fruit once again. If the God of heaven was willing to hold back natural forces that produce rain and then once again bring about the rain because of Elijah's prayer, will He not also grant prayers today if one prays an effectual fervent prayer according to His will?

5:19—Brethren, If Any Of You Do Err From The Truth, And One Convert Him

Should a fellow believer "err from the truth" doctrinally or fall into sinful practices, he would need restoring. James is encouraging all faithful believers to be their brother's keeper. One erring is heading in the wrong direction and straying or wandering from the sheep away from the safety of the fold. "And one convert him" means to restore him to the truth. Paul also similarly addressed the faithful individuals from the churches of Galatia, "Brethren, if a man be overtaken in a fault, ye which are spiritual, restore such a one in the spirit of meekness; considering thyself, lest thou also be tempted. Bear ye one another's burdens, and so fulfil the law of Christ" (Gal. 6:1, 2). Jesus stated that it is the "truth" that can set one free (John 8:32). In the N.T., many other inspired writers have written of our responsibilities to admonish those who are turning from the path of light to darkness. What a great honor it is in the following verse to convert one from error to righteousness!

5:20—Let Him Know, That He Which Converteth The Sinner From The Error Of His Way Shall Save A Soul From Death, And Shall Hide A Multitude Of Sins

All faithful believers are encouraged to be soul winners. James commands faithful brethren: "Let him know" what an honor it is to convert and save another person's soul from eternal death. By doing such, it shall hide a multitude of sins that the sinner has committed. Restoring a brother reminds us of our loving God, Who is "not willing that any should perish, but that all should come to repentance" (2 Peter 3:9). Jude 23 says, "And others save with fear, pulling them out of the fire." Snatching them out of the fire of hell or rescue them from the danger of destruction.

"And shall hide a multitude of sins" in this verse means that the rescued person's sins will be blotted out, cleansed by the blood of Jesus. The reason James shows it is important to win a soul back to Christ because one can "save a soul from death." Death is spiritual death!

Contrary to what some denominations believe and teach, a saved person can stray away from Christ and be eternally lost. Study very carefully Hebrew 6:1-6. Peter states in 2 Peter 2:20-22, "For if after they have escaped the pollutions of the world through the knowledge of the Lord and Saviour Jesus Christ, they are again entangled therein, and overcome, the latter end is worse with them than the beginning. For it had been better for them not to have known the way of righteousness, than, after they have known it, to turn from the holy commandment delivered unto them. But it is happened unto them according to the true proverb, The dog is turned to his own vomit again; and the sow that was washed to her wallowing in the mire."

Once an erring child of God has been restored to the Lord, the blood of Jesus once again covers his sins (1 John 1:7). The phrase "shall hide a multitude of sins" implies forgiveness. Read Psalm 32:1; 51:1-12; Acts 8:9-13, 18-25; Romans 4:7. Truly, when the blood of Jesus covers one's sins, his multitude of sins are washed away unless he falls away from his steadfastness (2 Peter 3:17).

Lesson Twelve Review Questions For Discussion (5:13-20)

Verse 13

1. Why does James instruct Christians to pray when afflicted and sing when merry?

_____

_____

Verse 14

2. Why are the sick instructed to call for those who hold the office of elders? ___

_____

_____

3. What is the purpose of anointing the sick with oil? _____

_____

Verse 15

4. What is the "prayer of faith?" _____

_____

5. Identify God's part and man's part regarding the sick overcoming their illness.

_____

_____

Verse 16

6. What is the significance of confessing our faults one to another and praying for one another? _____

_____

_____

7. Describe an effectual and fervent prayer. _____

_____

_____

Verse 17

8. What does it mean that a Christian and Elijah have "like passions?" _____

_____

_____

_____

Verse 18

9. What shows the effectiveness of Elijah's prayer? _____

_____

_____

Verse 19

10. What does it mean to err from the truth? _____

_____

11. Who is responsible for converting those brethren in error? _____

_____

Verse 20

12. What is the result of converting a sinner from the error of their way? _____

_____

_____

13. How does 2 Peter 3:9 relate to what James is discussing here. _____

_____

_____

A BIBLIOGRAPHY OF STUDY MATERIALS
ON THE EPISTLE OF JAMES

The Bible student that desires a further study of the Epistle of James may want to consult the following commentaries, expositions, and dictionaries. While studying the Epistle of James, I found the following scholarly sources to be very helpful in aiding my understanding while writing a verse by verse commentary of this marvelous book. Always remember the Bible must be one's final guide into all truth. It is written, "All scripture is given by inspiration of God, and is profitable for doctrine, for reproof, for correction, for instruction in righteousness: That the man of God may be perfect, thoroughly furnished unto all good works" (2 Tim. 3:16-17).

Commentaries on the Book of James

• Adams, Wilson James. *The Case for Practical Christianity*. AlphaGraphics, 2015.
• *Barnes Notes Heritage Edition*. Blackie & Son, 1884.
• Billingsley, Rick. *The Book of James*. Guardian of Truth Foundation Athens, 2014.
• Caton, N.T. *A Commentary and Exposition of the Epistle of James*. E. S. Smith, publisher, 1897.
• Harkrider, Robert. *Galatians and James, Legalism versus Liberty*. Impressive Image Production.
• Strong, James. *Strong's Exhaustive Concordance with Hebrew, Chaldee and Greek Dictionaries*. Mac Donald Publishing Company.
• Tolle, James M. *Notes on James*. Haun Publishing Company, 1975.
• Vine, W.E. *Vine's Expository Dictionary of N.T. Words*. MacDonald Publishing Company.

Made in the USA
Monee, IL
03 July 2020